PICTURING *the* FACE *of* JESUS

PICTURING *the* FACE *of* JESUS

ENCOUNTERING CHRIST THROUGH ART

BETH BOORAM

Abingdon Press
Nashville

PICTURING THE FACE OF JESUS
ENCOUNTERING CHRIST THROUGH ART

This book is printed on acid-free paper.

Library of Congress Cataloging-in-Publication Data

Booram, Beth.
  Picturing the face of Jesus : encountering Christ through art / Beth Booram.
     p.   cm.
  ISBN 978-0-687-65743-8 (pbk. : alk. paper)
  1. Jesus Christ—Face.   2. Jesus Christ—Art.   I. Title.

BT590.P45B66   2009
232.9—dc22

2009003069

09 10 11 12 13 14 15 16 17 18—10 9 8 7 6 5 4 3 2 1

MANUFACTURED IN THE UNITED STATES OF AMERICA

To the kind and generous people of
Christ the Savior Lutheran Church,
Fishers, Indiana,
and especially my friend and colleague,
Pastor Joseph M. Freeman

CONTENTS

ACKNOWLEDGMENTS

"Picturing the Face of Jesus" was an Advent series that I developed during my first year as an interim minister at Christ the Savior Lutheran Church (CTS) in Fishers, Indiana. I am indebted to Pastor Joe Freeman, my fellow staff members, and the many wonderful people from CTS who opened their hearts to me.

Thank you to the staff at Abingdon Press for your caring and professional support that made this project possible, color images and all!

I am grateful to Judy Keene for her generous gift as a writing coach. (I just rewrote the previous sentence so that it wouldn't end with a prepositional phrase.)

To my faithful prayer team—bless you for your gracious support and ministry prayers as I travel and speak.

Profound thanks to my C.O.T. (Circle of Trust): Mary, Pam, Jan, and Sandee—for your trusted and faithful companionship.

Finally, to my loving and amazing family: my incredible soul mate—David; my extraordinary daughters—Britt, Bri, and Brooke; and my exceptional son, Brandt, and his delightful new bride, Laura.

INTRODUCTION

For God, who said, "Let there be light in the darkness,"
has made this light shine in our hearts so we could
know the glory of God that is seen in the face
of Jesus Christ.
—2 Corinthians 4:6

THE FACE OF JESUS

Have you ever wondered what Jesus looked like? Have you ever tried to imagine his face?

I have. I've tried, in my mind's eye, to picture him. If Jesus were in a crowd of people, would I be able to pick him out? If he walked up and said hello, would I recognize him? I have imagined seeing Jesus for the very first time and wondered if there would be something so familiar, so distinguishable or maybe even haunting, that I would immediately know it was him.

The truth is Jesus had a one-of-a-kind, unmistakable face. Yet, we don't have a shred of description about what he looked like! None of the Gospel writers included any details of Jesus' physical stature or appearance. Even art historians come up empty-handed regarding any authentic first-century portraits of Christ.

Though we don't know what Jesus looked like, we do know that those who met him during his life on earth saw his face. They gazed into the very eyes of the Son of God. If we could talk to these people and ask them, they would be able to describe the face of Christ. With their words, they could sketch the features that defined the memorable human face of Jesus.

THE ALLURE OF THE HUMAN FACE

Jesus isn't the only one who has a distinctive human face. So does every person alive today. Each individual's face is the single most expressive, unique feature of his or her physical body.

Sir Thomas Browne, a seventeenth-century English author, wrote, "It is the common wonder of all men, how among so many millions of faces, there should be none alike." And centuries later, with more than six billion people inhabiting our world, we feel the same wonder.

Think about it: your face is the focal point of your connection with other people. You engage others with your facial expressions. When you communicate, you use your features—especially your eyes. They relay unspoken messages, ones that convey your deepest thoughts and feelings.

Even newborn babies, within the first nine minutes of birth and barely able to focus their eyes on anything, will focus on a human face. They clumsily search to find the eyes belonging to the voice that has become familiar to them while in the womb. Nothing on the planet will hold a baby's gaze like its mother's face!

A WINDOW INTO OUR HEARTS

Not only is a person's countenance alluring, it is a window into his or her heart. The writer of Proverbs says that "Just as water mirrors your face, / so your face mirrors your heart" (Proverbs 27:19, *The Message*). The expressions we wear on our face divulge what we think and feel deep within us.

We learn to study people's faces to help us discern their character and disposition. We read their nonverbal expressions to determine what they think of us. We rely on their faces to provide the vital information we need to help us navigate a relationship with them.

If, indeed, the face is so critical to human connection, communication, and trust, then it seems obvious that connecting with God, face-to-face, is extremely important in order for us to experience meaningful conversation and authentic relationship with him.

THE FACE OF GOD

Even God has a face. The Bible describes God's face as the central point of access and connection with him. We are told to "seek God's face"; that he will "make his face shine upon us." We're warned that when we turn away from God, that he will "hide his face from us" and "set his face against us."

This metaphoric language describes God's face as an entrée into personal engagement with him: When we seek his face, we are seeking a personal encounter with him. When God hides his face from us, he holds back from communicating with us. If God sets his face against us, he purposefully opposes us.

Moses was a man privileged to become familiar with God's face. He would meet with God in a tent outside the Israelite camp. There, God would speak to Moses, "face to face, as a man speaks with his friend" (Exodus 33:11 NIV). This expression conjures up a picture of two confidants conversing in comfortable, self-disclosing dialogue.

PICTURING THE FACE OF JESUS

Over the centuries, artists have tried to capture Christ's face on canvas. Painters from each period of history depicted him in a stylized way that they, in their cultural context, envisioned him. Several of the images of Jesus were iconic. Other artists strived for a realistic version of Christ. Some produced a historical Jesus, yet others represented the cosmic Christ. Many artists illustrated him with European features, though some painted him with more authentic Middle Eastern traits. Each artist's rendering is his or her attempt to picture the face of Jesus.

I remember the first picture of Jesus that ever caught my attention. It was in my best friend's home, during grade school. The first time I visited Cheryl, I spotted this portrait of Christ hanging conspicuously on a wall in her living room.

It made a profound impression on me, as I had never before seen Jesus' picture on display in a home. I was both drawn to the image and uncomfortable with it. I deduced that Cheryl's family must be very religious—Jesus, someone I knew little about, was obviously important to them. Whenever we played in the living room, I was aware of Christ's company, a mystifying presence, a sort of proctor, keeping us on good behavior.

Though we may have a favorite portrait of Jesus, it is unlikely we will see what Jesus truly looked like until we meet him face-to-face. However, there is an imaginative way to picture his face. If we read the Gospel stories, paying attention to the way people experienced Christ, we can learn a great deal about what it was like to peer into the face of the Son of God.

These Gospel stories describe people who met Jesus in the midst of their ordinary lives. When they encountered him, they heard him speak, they felt his touch, they experienced his personhood, and they read the human expressions on his face.

These people didn't just hear what Jesus was saying, they responded to his emotional effect. Beyond his words, he spoke to them through his expressive countenance. They peered into his eyes as if through a window into his soul. They tasted something real in Jesus—his welcoming heart, his longing gaze, his indignant anger, his empathy seasoned through suffering. His heart frequently bled through to his face and often disarmed them, which is why so many responded as dramatically to him as they did.

THE EQ OF JESUS

Jesus had a high "EQ" or Emotional Intelligence Quotient. It's undeniable that there was something powerful and magnetic about his emotional impact. He perceived, understood, and expressed feelings in the most articulate way. He possessed the ability to console people by offering a genuine empathy that was irresistible. The evidence of Jesus' EQ lies in the fact that such a wide variety of individuals—from timid introverts to hardened characters—found his company inviting.

In the Gospel stories, Jesus exuded a wide array of feelings. He got angry—hot-under-the-collar angry. He was doubled over with gut-wrenching sorrow. He brimmed with warm compassion and seethed with indignation.

Jesus was fully alive, fully human, and expressed a full range of emotions that offered those in his company a taste of his authentic humanity and divinity. His emotional intelligence brought his heart to the surface and generated trust and connection with those he engaged. Consequently, his face became one they could trust.

REAL JESUS

Most of us have heard much about the truth and teachings of Jesus. He is often lifted up as a historical figure—important to follow as an example but not very accessible as a person. While living in the way and truth of Jesus are essential to our faith, nothing can replace our need to reencounter the real Jesus, again and again, throughout our lifetime.

If we lose the sense of his realness and humanity, his personhood and presence, following Christ can become simply the next faddish cause to join or lifestyle to adopt. That is why envisioning Jesus' face—his expressive, one-of-a-kind, human face, is invaluable. It protects him from becoming merely an admired archetype rather than a real person.

Picturing the face of Jesus is an opportunity to reimagine the face of Christ—to peer into it as a mirror that reflects his heart. The possibility of this reenvisioning is based upon four tenets.

First, Jesus has a real, human face; and his face is a window into the nature of his heart. Cultivating an imagination for Christ's expressions as he was encountered by people in the Gospels helps him become more three-dimensional to us. Reading beneath Jesus' words to his influence on individuals provides rich detail to the narrative of his life.

Second, focusing on and observing the face of Jesus can begin to heal our image of God. We all carry snapshots in our mind of what we think God is like. Some of those images, though perhaps subconscious, are distorted and marred. Some are fantasies. Some are propaganda. Through envisioning the face of Christ, our image of God, made known through Christ, is re-formed.

Third, as we encounter Jesus' face, we are nurtured and transformed through that encounter. By imagining and meditating on his countenance, we gain knowledge of him that moves beyond our heads, into our heart. We take him in more deeply and personally; his presence becomes more real. *Radical faith is born from real encounter.*

Fourth, through this encounter and transformation, we begin to mirror Jesus' face as we engage with others. You know what it is like to be influenced by someone you admire. You take them in, and what you experience from them changes you. You begin to emulate the unconditional love and unbiased acceptance you received from them. That's how it works when we spend time with Jesus, face-to-face.

A PATHWAY OF TRANSFORMATION

The Gospel stories that we will consider illustrate the veracity of this pathway of transformation. The individuals in these stories saw the face of Christ and were changed, much like the transformation described in 2 Corinthians 3:16-18 from *The Message*:

> Whenever, though, they turn to face God as Moses did, God removes the veil and there they are—face-to-face! They suddenly recognize that God is a living, personal presence, not a piece of chiseled stone. And when God is personally present, a living Spirit, that old, constricting legislation is recognized as obsolete. We're free of it! All of us! Nothing between us and God, our faces shining with the brightness of his face. And so we are transfigured much like the Messiah, our lives gradually becoming brighter and more beautiful as God enters our lives and we become like him.

ART CONTEMPLATION—A MEDIUM OF TRANSFORMATION

Provocative art is one medium through which we can meditate on Christ's face. Art communicates truth in a way that words cannot. In a day when we are constantly bombarded with information and overstimulated by massive amounts of words, art is a much-needed, soul-nourishing medium of transformation.

You will find eight images in the center of this book. Six of them relate to one chapter each and capture that particular expression on the face of Christ. Before you read the chapter, begin by taking several minutes to contemplate the corresponding piece of art. I encourage you to listen to some quiet, reflective music as you meditate. Take as long as you desire, prayerfully studying the face of Christ and opening your heart to him.

Following your contemplation on the art, you will be invited to turn to the chapter, write about your reflections on the image, and then read the corresponding chapter.

Each chapter will conclude with a section inviting you to enter the gospel story through imagining prayer. Through guided instruction, you will place yourself in the story as the featured individual with whom Christ engaged. You will picture Jesus responding to you as he did to this person. You will be invited to witness the same expression that Jesus offered when this person encountered his face.

Following each chapter you will find some questions for reflection and conversation. These questions can be helpful for your own spiritual process and as a prompt for small-group interaction.

FEELING VULNERABLE

Looking into another person's face makes us feel vulnerable. It's hard to do when we don't know that person well or when we feel like hiding. It's uncomfortable when we're angry and out of sorts, or when we don't trust him or her. For these reasons, spending time face-to-face with Jesus can make us feel anxious.

If that is true for you, you may want to begin by telling Jesus exactly how you feel. Tell him about your fears and apprehensions. Tell him why you want to run away. The best place to begin is with honesty about the things that get in the way of your spending time, face-to-face, with Christ.

Art contemplation and imagining prayer may both be new and unfamiliar spiritual practices for you. Don't be afraid to use your imagination. Be open to the transformation that comes through meditating on the face of Christ in these ways, and welcome his presence through this sacred pathway. As you do, may your own face become brighter and more beautiful, as you see and reflect the glory of God in the face of Jesus Christ.

HEAD OF CHRIST
BY REMBRANDT

If you are new to the practice of art contemplation, you may want to begin with an introductory exercise of meditating on an image of Christ. Keep in mind there is no right or wrong way to respond to art. Using your own skills of observation, make note of what stands out to you and validate your own interpretations.

The cover image of Jesus was painted by Rembrandt in the seventeenth century and can also be found as illustration 7. Spend several minutes reflecting on this rendering of Christ and respond to the following questions.

How would you describe the expression on Jesus' face? What is he feeling?

Describe your reactions to Jesus' expression.

Where are your eyes drawn?

In what ways do you connect with this face of Jesus?

In what ways do you not connect with this face of Jesus?

THE FACE OF WELCOME

ART CONTEMPLATION

Turn to illustration 1 and spend several minutes contemplating Jesus' face of welcome.

Describe your reactions to this scene of Jesus with these children.

Where are your eyes drawn?

With which child do you most identify?

As you study the face of Jesus, how would you describe his expression? How does his face make you feel?

CHAPTER ONE

THE FACE OF WELCOME

He called a little child and had him stand among them.
And he said . . . "Whoever welcomes a little child like
this in my name welcomes me."
—*Matthew 18:2, 5 NIV*

WELCOME HOME

When you think of someone with a welcoming face, who comes to mind? A grandmother welcoming you home for the holidays? Your kids welcoming you at the door after a long day's work? The welcome of a good friend you haven't seen in quite a while? There's nothing more heartening than to be greeted by a face of welcome, a face that says, "I'm so glad to see you!"

I have a distinct memory of such a welcome. Several years ago, when my father was in the late stages of terminal cancer, my mother went through her own cancer scare. For obvious reasons, both of my parents were a mess. Uncertain of the outcome of Mom's biopsy (thankfully, it was benign!), and facing the devastating outcome of Dad's illness and eventual death, they were jolted by the cruelty of this indiscriminate disease.

I was staying with Dad when Mom came home from the hospital after her surgery. He had been waiting anxiously for hours for her return. As she walked in the door, Dad lifted his eyes to her, his face washed with relief.

He struggled to push himself up from his chair and hobbled forward. Mom slowly and gingerly shuffled toward him. Their faces beamed with absolute delight at the sight of each other. In the middle of the room, they met, wrapping each other in a tender embrace. I sat watching it all, blinking away tears, privileged to witness the profound love my parents shared.

THE MESSAGE OF A WELCOMING FACE

What is the message you read when you are greeted by someone's welcoming face? Is it the message of warmth? Or gladness? Or receptivity? A welcoming face is filled with reassurance and conveys an unspoken message that you matter. Someone who greets you with this expression extends hospitality and conveys his or her desire for relationship.

On the other hand, an unwelcoming face is quick to snuff out any presumption of meaningful relationship. It transmits feelings of disapproval and rejection. If you've ever experienced feeling unwelcome, it's one of the most awkward and uncomfortable moments ever—one that prompts you to look desperately for the nearest escape route.

I experienced such a situation several years ago when my husband and I were on vacation. Through the generous gift of a friend, we spent several days in her golf-course condominium. The day we arrived, we went straight from the airport to the clubhouse to pick up a pass in order to enter this gated community. We were dressed in jeans, comfortable clothes for traveling.

We approached the welcome desk and introduced ourselves. I was keenly aware of the stiffness and formality of the woman who helped us. I glanced around the palatial surroundings. The furnishings were exquisite.

After receiving our pass, the woman also handed me another slip of paper. I looked at it curiously. It read, "No denim, please." I glanced back, her eyes avoiding mine, and we abruptly slunk away. As far as I was concerned, we couldn't get out of there quickly enough!

THE WELCOME ON JESUS' FACE

Do you envision Jesus with a welcoming face? Think about the times when he welcomed children—children who were squirmy, had dirty hands, and who said and did unpredictable things. As in the art you viewed for this chapter, Jesus scooped the children up onto his lap. He warned his disciples not to interfere with their access to him. He said the kingdom of heaven belonged especially to them.

Jesus was known (and criticized) for welcoming those who were least valued in his world—the misfits and marginalized. He reached out to the sick, the lepers, and those possessed by demons. He was a friend to widows and women. The Gospels trace numerous occasions when tax collectors and notorious sinners were welcomed to share the intimacy of a meal with Jesus and his disciples.

Jesus also told "welcome home" stories. He offered a parable where a father received home his wayward son— one who had deserted the family and squandered his inheritance on reckless living. Relaying the story, Jesus said that while the son was still a long way off, the father saw his son "and was filled with compassion for him; he ran to his son, threw his arms around him and kissed him" (Luke 15:20 NIV). Like the ending of a great movie, this final scene in Jesus' story captures the glory of a celebrated homecoming!

It is apparent from these examples that many people who met Jesus were greeted by his welcoming face. And it explains, in part, why people responded as they did. People found him so naturally disarming. Jesus' face convinced them that he was approachable, that he accepted them. Often, we find Jesus extending generous invitations to those least likely to be on anyone's invitation list. One of those unlikely characters was named Zacchaeus (see Luke 19:1-10).

AN UNEXPECTED INVITATION

Jesus was passing through the town of Jericho one day. He was with his disciples and seemed to have every intention to keep heading toward Jerusalem, until something happened that caught his attention. He met a man named Zacchaeus, a well-known, well-to-do man.

Zacchaeus was well known because he had the infamous job of being a tax collector. And he was well-to-do not just because he was a tax collector but also because he was the *chief* tax collector. He had many people working for him.

As Jesus made his way through the town, a crowd began to gather and follow along with him. There must have been quite a throng, because Zacchaeus, determined as he was, couldn't edge his way close enough to get a good look at Jesus. Part of the problem was the fact that he was uncommonly short.

But Zacchaeus was also resourceful. He knew the route Jesus was taking and spotted a familiar tree up ahead. It was a tree Zacchaeus had walked by almost every day of his life—sometimes several times a day. But it is unlikely he had ever before considered it to be such a perfect perch!

Zacchaeus, short-legged and stocky, hoisted himself up onto a low limb and climbed a few branches up so he could get a good look. From his new birds'-eye position, Zacchaeus had Jesus in clear view. But it never occurred to him that Jesus also would have an improved vantage point to see him.

Suddenly, the crowds halted. Jesus pressed his way through the middle, his eyes intent on Zacchaeus. He kept his gaze high as he approached the tree. His face had an expression of amusement and pleasure. And then he spoke. He told Zacchaeus to come down, right now, because he wanted to have lunch at Zacchaeus's house! Zacchaeus was flabbergasted. He scooted down from the tree and welcomed Jesus to come home with him.

The atmosphere among the crowd turned sour. Filled with disgust and incredulity, they murmured to one another, loathing the idea that Jesus was going to visit the home of a "sinner."

A LEAST-LIKELY CHARACTER

Zacchaeus lived in Jericho, a city that was about seventeen miles from Jerusalem and a mile south of the Old Testament's Jericho (whose walls came tumbling down, as the song goes). Bordering Judea and Samaria, it had a sizeable customs station to accommodate the heavy commerce passing between the two countries. Jericho was one of the wealthiest cities in Palestine, located as it was in the most fertile part of Judea. It was a lucrative place for a tax collector to live.

Zacchaeus was a Jew who was hired by the Roman government to collect taxes from his fellow citizens. Because tax collectors would have to make up any financial shortfall to the Roman government, they were often hard-nosed, conniving, and greedy, exacting more taxes than were actually due.

Moreover, as a chief tax collector, Zacchaeus skimmed a portion of the taxes collected by those reporting to him. It is no surprise that most Jewish citizens had contempt for tax collectors. They were viewed as traitors and conspirators, siding with a government the Jews detested.

It was this man, slight in stature and short on integrity, who received an unexpected invitation: lunch with the Rabbi! From his cloistered nook in a tree, this cynical little man looked down. To his surprise, his eyes met the pleasure of Jesus' welcoming face.

A WELCOMED INTERRUPTION

Luke, the writer of this story, tells us that Jesus was passing through Jericho. It appears that his intention was to continue on without stopping to pay a visit. However, those plans were abandoned when Jesus looked up into a tree, noticed this grown man lodged in its branches, and invited himself over for lunch.

When someone is a welcoming person, that quality is often seen in his or her willingness to be interrupted. Hospitable people view others as more important than their "to do" lists. They are willing to set aside their plans to accommodate an unexpected visitor. Whatever Jesus had planned, he gave it up for the opportunity to engage with this peculiar little man.

WELCOMING HIMSELF

Under any circumstance, inviting oneself to a stranger's home was a highly unusual gesture. During the first century, not unlike today, it was proper for the host to do the inviting. Can you imagine how the proposition hit Zacchaeus?

When people invite themselves over to your home, how does that make you feel? It might depend on who they are! But generally, it says that they are familiar and comfortable with you; like you are family. Their overture presumes openness and receptivity on your part.

Jesus' initiative undoubtedly caught Zacchaeus off-guard. He probably hadn't gotten many requests like this, much less from a rabbi. In spite of his cynicism, Jesus' appeal probably made Zacchaeus feel special, desirable, and pursued. You can imagine it must have opened his heart toward Jesus, because this wasn't the way he was used to being treated.

Not only did Jesus express an overture of friendship toward Zacchaeus, he asked Zacchaeus to meet his needs. Jesus was tired and hungry and needed a place to rest and be fed.

It takes humility on our part when we ask someone for help. By requesting that Zacchaeus care for him, Jesus was expressing an attitude of mutuality. In turn, Zacchaeus was given honor by being invited to meet the needs of someone as important as Jesus.

COME AS YOU ARE, WHOEVER YOU ARE

Now think about the scene from Jesus' perspective. As he was passing through Jericho, crowds of people pressing in around him, he looked up and saw a man perched in the crook of a tree—a sight that would have been hard not to notice.

Evidently, Jesus was amused and impressed and called Zacchaeus down by name. It's unclear how Jesus knew Zacchaeus' name, or for that matter, whether Jesus knew anything else about him—like the fact that he was a shrewd tax collector and swindler.

But one thing is clear, Jesus didn't seem to care. His request was a "come as you are, whoever you are" request. He singled Zacchaeus out of the crowd because he liked what he saw—a man with the gumption to overcome any obstacle in his way in order to see Jesus.

Zacchaeus must have heard the crowd murmuring their objections, projecting the same disgust that he was all too used to receiving. No honorable Jewish person, let alone a rabbi, ever gave him respectful notice. To hear that this rabbi, Jesus, wanted to come to his home and share a meal was astonishing!

Now, pause for a moment and imagine Zacchaeus taking Jesus in. Zacchaeus looks into his face and reads his non-verbal expressions. He observes Jesus' manner, his countenance, and his tone. What he experiences is enough to persuade him not only to agree to host an unplanned dinner party, but to later inspire him to become wildly generous and make major restitution to those he had cheated.

THE HEART BEHIND A FACE OF WELCOME

If Jesus' face of welcome is a mirror of his heart, what attitudes cultivated this disposition? At the heart of welcome is an attitude of generosity. When Jesus looked at Zacchaeus, he felt a warmth and responsiveness. He saw him as a valuable human being, rather than a despicable man.

Jesus saw beyond Zacchaeus's sordid vocation, into his heart. He viewed him as a person with worth. To Christ, Zacchaeus wasn't defined by his sin and brokenness, but by his dignity as a human being. Jesus recognized in him a heart that needed to be watered with love and genuine interest. He felt compassion, not pity; possibilities, not deficit.

THE TRANSFORMATION FROM A GRACIOUS WELCOME

Picture Zacchaeus's home packed with people—undoubtedly other tax collectors and riff-raff, because they were the only friends Zacchaeus would have had. Imagine Jesus reclined at a low table. Dinner served, the conversation began crisscrossing around the table.

Then suddenly, Zacchaeus springs to his feet. All eyes are on him. He clears his throat and announces, in a loud voice, that he plans to give half of his possessions to the poor and to pay back anyone he has cheated by four times the amount. At this point, the crowd might have wondered if Zacchaeus had too much to drink. It wouldn't have been the first time. Privately, they probably doubted his sincerity.

But Jesus didn't respond this way. He affirmed Zacchaeus with unquestioning faith.

Jesus celebrated Zacchaeus's transformation. He likened it to a common image—a lost sheep that had found its way home. He announced to the dinner party that Zacchaeus, a "son of Abraham" (a reference that would have made many Jews flinch), had been brought back into the fold. Jesus further declared that this was his mission—to seek and to welcome back home those who had been lost.

Jesus offered Zacchaeus a relationship of shameless and unreserved acceptance. Clearly, the expression of welcome on Jesus' face, a mirror of the receptivity in his heart, transformed this miserly man into a generous human being.

REFLECTING HIS FACE OF WELCOME

As you experience more of the responsive face of Christ, and as you are transformed by the love that he exudes through his unconditional reception of you, your own heart will be changed toward those who need your welcome.

What person comes to mind right now as someone who is difficult for you to receive into your life? What is it about him or her that turns you off? You might be expressing healthy boundaries with this person, which is important to do, especially if he or she is harmful or a bad influence on you. If not, are you rejecting someone who is different from you or simply hard for you to love?

What about this person, or this kind of person, do you object to or reject? What about them makes you feel uncomfortable? In prayer, ask the Holy Spirit to help you picture him or her in your mind and imagine offering this person a friendly face. Find in your own heart the greeting that you have received from Christ and offer his welcome to him or her.

EXPRESSING WELCOME THROUGH HOSPITALITY

My friend Laurie has a way of welcoming people into her life and home like no one else I know. She notices everyone. She never meets a stranger, whether on an airplane or in the grocery store.

A few months ago, Laurie was out with her family. They had pizza at a favorite spot in Broad Ripple, an artsy district in Indianapolis. After dinner, they were walking back to their car and passed by some "bridge kids"—homeless teenagers who hang out on a bridge over the canal that flows through Broad Ripple.

Laurie recognized the group of kids from a conversation she'd had with them earlier that week. She walked up and began to talk. Before you know it, she mentioned that her birthday was the next day, and that she would love to celebrate by having them over to her home for a good home-cooked meal.

The next evening, Laurie, her daughter, and her daughter-in-law picked up six of these kids and brought them to her home. Laurie lit candles and set fresh flowers on the table. She served them on her best china. And she fed them a feast in celebration of all their own birthdays that had been missed.

On each of their chairs she had placed a backpack, stuffed with food, toiletries, and new socks and underwear. Laurie said she would rather use her birthday money on these kids than on herself.

Laurie welcomed them into her heart and home. She mirrored the face of Jesus, as she practiced hospitality. She embodied the generous, nonjudging, receptive attitudes of a welcoming person. Laurie was Jesus to them.

IMAGINING PRAYER: LETTING JESUS WELCOME YOU

When you picture Jesus' face, do you imagine it as an inviting one? When you pray, do you feel a sense of warmth in his presence? Do you long to experience him as the receptive, open, and responsive person whom Zacchaeus experienced?

If so, begin by imagining and meditating on the story of Zacchaeus. Thoughtfully read the story in Luke 19:1-10 a few times.

- In prayer, picture yourself crouched on the limb of that tree. Why is it important for you to see Jesus?

- Imagine the crowd parting, and Jesus looking up at you with an expression of openness and delight. What does it feel like to be greeted by his welcoming face?
- Allow the goodness of his warmth toward you, the smile on his face, to warm your heart. Respond in whatever way feels natural to you.
- Meditate on the sensation of Jesus' welcoming face as he greets you. You may not picture an actual face, but rather feel the gladness embodied in his expression.
- Have a conversation with Jesus. Stay in the tree as long as you need to be there. When you are ready, accept his request to come home with you. Open your heart to his welcoming presence and simply be with him.

QUESTIONS FOR PERSONAL REFLECTION OR SMALL GROUP INTERACTION

1. Take a moment, and in quiet prayer and reflection, ask God to bring to your conscious mind a tree that has been significant to you. Write about that tree and what it means to you.

2. When you think of someone who has a welcoming face, what person comes to mind? Describe that person.

3. Why do you think it was so important for Zacchaeus to see Jesus?

4. How would you describe what Zacchaeus must have felt when he saw Jesus' face?

5. In the past, have you envisioned Jesus with a welcoming face? Explain.

6. Picture yourself in the tree that you envisioned earlier. Imagine Jesus walking up to the tree and looking up at you. What do you think he would say? What would you like for him to say?

THE FACE OF COMPASSION

ART CONTEMPLATION

Turn to illustration 2 and take several minutes to contemplate Jesus' face of compassion.

Describe your reactions to the interpersonal dynamics between Jesus and this woman.

Where are your eyes drawn?

In what way do you identify with this expression on Jesus' face?

As you study the face of Jesus, how would you describe his expression? How does his face make you feel?

CHAPTER TWO

THE FACE OF COMPASSION

When he saw the crowds, he had compassion on them
because they were confused and helpless, like sheep
without a shepherd.
—*Matthew 9:36*

THE ART OF COMPASSION

O. Henry, an American writer known for his masterful short story "The Gift of the Magi," also wrote a lesser-known piece called "The Last Leaf," replete with the O. Henry signature ending—an unexpected twist. Here is a paraphrase of the story.

"The Last Leaf" tells of two women, Sue and Johnsy, living in New York City's Greenwich Village. They were young and poor, residing in an apartment building with other hand-to-mouth occupants. One of those residents was an artist, an older man who lived beneath them whose name was Behrman. To call him an artist was really a misnomer. He was a failure as a painter—always about to paint a masterpiece, though he had never even begun one.

The story is cast during a time when pneumonia was often epidemic and fatal. Tragically, Johnsy became ill with the disease, and her condition deteriorated rapidly.

She spent her days in bed, looking out the window where she could see a single ivy vine on the brick house next door. It was November, and the biting wind began to strip off the leaves in a fury. Each day, Johnsy watched as the vine lost more and more of its foliage.

One day, she told Sue that "when the last leaf falls, I must go, too."

"I've never heard of such nonsense," complained Sue. But for Johnsy, the vine was an omen.

She became increasingly frail as the vine outside her window became more bare. One morning she awoke and there was only one leaf left. Behrman stopped by for his daily visit, and Sue showed him Johnsy's vine with the single leaf hanging.

The leaf helped her keep vigil. Though the day was gray and windy, the leaf hung on. Night came and went, and the next morning Johnsy awoke, certain to find a barren vine. To her surprise, the last leaf was still there. It gave her renewed hope; maybe she would hang on, as well.

Remarkably, the next day the leaf was still there, and Johnsy clearly felt better, her strength gaining. Then, after a few days passed and her recovery was certain, Sue told Johnsy the awful news: Behrman had caught pneumonia and died. The janitor found him in his apartment, soaked to the bone and icy cold. They couldn't imagine where he had been until they found a ladder, a lantern, and brushes dabbled with green and yellow paint.

"Look out the window, dear, at the last ivy leaf on the wall. Didn't you wonder why it never fluttered or moved when the wind blew? Ah, darling, it's Behrman's masterpiece—he painted it there the night that the last leaf fell."

THE MESSAGE ON A COMPASSIONATE FACE

There is nothing more soothing to a hurting heart then the gift of a friend's compassion. Like this story of the benevolent artist, whose daily visits and ultimate act of kindness sustained this woman, other stories abound.

You've heard them—soldiers who were kept alive through the attention of a caring nurse, or a person afflicted with grief who was brought back to life by a concerned neighbor.

The word *compassion* is a beautiful word made of two parts: *com*, meaning "with," and *pati*, meaning "to suffer." Together the combination means to suffer with or alongside another. A compassionate individual identifies with others' pain so personally that it's as though he or she is feeling the pain with them. You read his or her expressive face: "I understand how badly you hurt, and I feel your misery with you." This caring friend offers you his or her healing company, a gift of empathic presence so that you are no longer alone in your difficulty.

Marilyn, my spiritual director, *oozes* compassion. The first time I met with her, I was deeply troubled and my heart racked with pain. I began to tell her what was going on, and I can still hear her saying, "Oh, honey. . . . Oh, honey." The tone of her voice was so sweet and responsive—it was healing in itself.

Compassion is not the same as pity. When we pity someone, we feel sorry for him or her, but we don't share in the person's pain. We aren't moved to act in order to alleviate his or her suffering. In "The Last Leaf," the artist didn't merely pity his young neighbor, he felt such deep concern for her that he couldn't help but act out of his tenderness toward her.

THE COMPASSIONATE FACE OF JESUS

Throughout the Gospels, Jesus always felt empathy when he encountered human suffering. "When he saw the crowds, he had compassion on them because they were confused and helpless, like sheep without a shepherd" (Matthew 9:36). When he stepped out of a boat and was greeted by a desperate crowd, "He had compassion on them and healed their sick" (Matthew 14:14). When he was with a large crowd for three days, he felt compassion for them because they were hungry (see Matthew 15:32).

Everywhere Jesus went, in his sensitivity he noticed pain in people's lives. He lived with such open responsiveness that when he saw another's hardship and suffering, he was right there, extending his heart.

That's what happened the day he was passing through Nain and found himself swept up in a funeral convoy. Instantly, Jesus was moved with compassion. He took one look at the mother of the dead man, who was also a widow, and promptly interjected himself into her story. (See Luke 7:11-17.)

ALWAYS ON CALL

As Jesus and his disciples traveled from Capernaum to the village of Nain, a large crowd began to follow along. They approached the city gate and noticed a commotion up ahead. Soon it became evident it was a funeral procession. It was a very large, solemn assembly, in route toward the burial site.

As was customary, the women, dressed in the drab garb of the grieving, walked ahead of the bier, which supported the body of the deceased person. All of them were crying pitifully. But clearly, one woman was most distressed. Her face was red and swollen, obviously from inconsolable tears. With head hung low, she whimpered with heart-wrenching forlornness.

Jesus honed in on the woman. He overheard those around him say that she was a widow and that the young man who had died was her only son. When Jesus saw her, "his heart overflowed with compassion" (Luke 7:13).

The scene immediately tapped into Jesus' deep reservoir of love and sympathy. Compiling all that he saw, felt empathically, and knew about her sounded an alarm within Jesus, awakening grave concern. It was evident that Jesus' heart of compassion was on call, ready to respond at any given moment.

His reaction, however, was not merely a superficial emotion. Jesus engaged with her in genuine empathy from his very nature. In a moment's notice, his tender heart received a dispatch. His response, however, was not a fleeting mood or whim.

Often, what we call and experience as compassion is no more than a pitying expression toward someone for whom we feel sorry. We hear a touching story or sad news, and we mimic empathic sounds. Yet, our response to the person or situation is often short-lived and rarely moves us toward thoughtful action.

"DON'T CRY"

Jesus instinctively stepped toward the mother and unintentionally interrupted the funeral procession—definitely a blatant breach in etiquette. He fixed his gaze upon her, her eyes lifting to distinguish the intruder; and Jesus blurted out, with strong passion, "Don't cry!"

What an odd thing to say to a woman who had just lost her only son. She was taken aback. Yet, as she locked onto Jesus' gaze, searching to place his face, she encountered such tenderness in his eyes that her heart softened. She could tell right away that his intentions were good.

Jesus' gentleness and warmth touched her; his sweet tone and understanding consoled her beyond words. It was obvious that his distress simply erupted in the most natural expression of comfort. "Don't cry" is what you say when you feel bad for someone and want to take away the sting.

Jesus couldn't bear to see this woman suffer. He intuitively knew how unbearable it was for a mother to lose a child—compounded when it is your only son. He also understood the social implications. As a widow with no son, this woman would be dependent on public charity for the rest of her life. Subsistence would be difficult.

The most natural desire of compassionate people is the desire to take away pain. They feel your hurt so deeply, as if it were *their* hurt, and everything within them wants to eliminate the affliction.

COMPASSION DOESN'T THINK TWICE

The young man had not been dead long. Burials had to take place quickly, in order to avoid the stench of decomposition. Those closest to the deceased had washed, anointed, and wrapped his body and had laid it in an open wooden frame in preparation for burial. Then, they carried his body through town, gathering people as they went along. It was customary for anyone, whether you knew the deceased or not, to drop whatever you were doing in order to join the procession. This town understood the unique tragedy of this young man's death—the only son of a widow—and gathered in full.

Then, Jesus, attuned to the extent of their grief, pressed through the crowd and "walked over to the coffin and touched it, and the bearers stopped" (Luke 7:14). The mother and those closest around her were appalled. Jesus' actions were shocking!

Anyone knew that touching a coffin or dead body exposed you to ritual uncleanness. According to Jewish law, corpse uncleanness was the severest form of impurity. If you didn't follow the laws of purification, you were cut off from the community of Israel.

Regardless, Jesus appeared to think nothing of it. He simply acted instinctively, and as a result, defiled himself. His compassion for this mother was such a strong force within him that he took a significant personal risk to act out of his concern.

RESTORING LIFE AND RELATIONSHIP

All eyes on Jesus, he called out to the lifeless figure, "Young man, I tell you, get up." For a swift moment, the mother and her entourage must have felt incredulous, until the dead boy on the bier sat up and began to talk! The throng stepped back in astonishment. The widow shrieked with pure joy and amazement, as Jesus "gave him back to his mother" (Luke 7:15).

Jesus, driven by tender impulse to restore life and relationship, resurrected this son to his mother. As the roots of a plant seek water, so the roots of compassion seek out ways of restoring life. Jesus coursed with determined commitment to return the boy to his mother's embrace—an ambition he was privileged to accomplish. His joy was second only to this mother's elation.

Her heart swelled with gratefulness, trying but unable to grasp the reality, hoping it wasn't a dream. At the same time, along with her, awe filled the crowd. What kind of man was this? A mighty prophet? Or had God come down from heaven and paid a visit?

THE HEART BEHIND COMPASSION

The compassionate face of Christ is a mirror of his heart, reflecting his genuine anguish over what causes us pain. Jesus truly hates death and all its ramifications. He reels with disconcertion when he sees suffering among the people he loves. Christ notices misery because it is such an affront to his desire for wholeness.

Yet, Jesus' ability to respond compassionately stems from his own secure, well-loved, and well-formed personhood. Because Jesus was whole within himself, his heart full of love and comfort from his Father, love spilled over toward this grieving widow.

Compassion is possible only when you are secure enough to lose yourself caring for another person. When you have a full and well-watered heart, you don't feel threatened by another's needs. You see the other as a separate entity and respond to him or her with regard and respect. You take the other in as he or she is—accepting, not judging, the person's condition.

That described Jesus' engagement with the widow. Rather than objectify, ignore, or act indifferently toward her, Jesus valued her, feeling compassion for her plight. She is one among a large cast of Gospel characters who reveal that meeting Jesus was an extraordinary experience. Every person felt important to Jesus because he gave them a rare and beautiful gift—the gift of his full and empathic presence.

THE TRANSFORMATION FROM COMPASSION

Jesus not only gave the woman back her son but also revived her hope. She tasted one of the transforming gifts of compassion—the renewal of expectancy and belief that life is good.

When hardship, loss, or suffering dampens a person's spirit, the presence of despair can be profound. Alone in his or her anguish, the discouraged forgets that life possesses beauty and that blessings still abound.

When a person extends tenderness and sympathy to the downtrodden, the effect is like ministering healing ointment, soothing and comforting to the heart like aloe on sunscorched skin. Through the gift of compassion, a hurting person regains courage to believe in life.

The first time I became pregnant, I miscarried the baby at fourteen weeks. This loss rocked my world. I will never forget the nurse who attended me. She was so gentle and spoke such consoling words of comfort. Her kindness helped me remember the blessedness of life and hope again in its possibilities.

REFLECTING COMPASSION

To reflect the compassion of Christ, you must first experience his transforming comfort in your own afflictions. Only then will you have a genuine capacity to extend yourself to others with healing kindness.

From your own encounter with Christ's tender mercy, you have a soothing gift to offer others who are living in pain. Whom do you know who has hurt in their eyes, or whose heart is broken? What person comes to mind who, like this widow, has suffered loss, felt destitute or hopeless? How can you be present to him or her?

As with the artist in the O. Henry story, one of the best gifts you can offer people who are hurting is to sit with them, contributing grace by listening to their story, and empathizing with their reality. Pray and ask God what "last leaf" of creativity, beauty, and sacrifice you can give to others.

EXPRESSING COMPASSION THROUGH VISITING

As a little girl, I would frequently "go visiting" with my grandmother. Apple pie in hand, Grandma would pick me up and take me with her as we visited the elderly, shut-ins, or people who needed cheering up.

One of the most memorable times was a visit to the home of a woman named Brownie. Brownie was blind. I recall feeling uneasy, not knowing how to act around a blind person. Her home looked quite normal, decorated, as well as tidy. She even had a grand piano in the living room— something I could never reconcile with her blindness.

Grandma and I would sit and chat. I don't recall the topic of the conversation. The apple pie was more memorable. Yet, I grew up believing that visiting was something you do—a normal, important service.

As a pastor, I now have many occasions to call on those who are sick, elderly, or need encouragement. It is some of my favorite work. The ministry of visiting is a wonderful way to practice compassion.

You can't be in a hurry when you visit. You must sit; listen; ask good questions; and consciously extend your heart to the person by empathizing with their myriad emotions—fear, frustration, anger, sorrow, or sadness.

Take a moment and consider someone who needs a visit. Slow down, sit with him or her (with or without apple pie), and extend comfort through the tender heart of Christ in you.

IMAGINING PRAYER: EXPERIENCING THE COMPASSION OF JESUS

Do you think of Jesus as having compassion for you? Do you envision him weeping with you over the hurts and disappointments in your life? Through imagining prayer, follow the steps of the widow and see what happens when you gaze upon Jesus' face of compassion.

- Read Luke 7:11-17 a few times, slowly and thoughtfully. Take some time to reflect on a loss that you are grieving right now. Feel the pain of it and imagine that loss on a funeral bier next to you.
- Now envision Jesus coming to you, looking into your eyes and saying, "Don't cry." Imagine the tender, kind expression on his face as he feels your loss. Picture Jesus' compassion poured into your heart like a warm, soothing balm. Let his healing come.
- Hear him say to your loss, "I tell you, get up." Contemplate what it means for him to revive what you have lost, to bring life out of death.
- Receive hope; imagine a new day dawning. Express your gratefulness to Jesus for his tender mercies.

QUESTIONS FOR PERSONAL REFLECTION OR SMALL GROUP INTERACTION

1. Take a moment, and in quiet prayer and reflection, ask God to bring to your conscious mind a time that was

particularly significant when you felt compassion from someone in your life. Write about that experience.

2. When you think of someone who is compassionate, who comes to mind? Describe that person.

3. What do you think it was like for this widow to see Jesus bring her dead son to life? Put yourself in her place and describe your emotions.

4. How would you describe what this woman must have felt when she looked into Jesus' face filled with compassion?

5. In the past, have you imagined Jesus being compassionate toward you? Explain.

6. Picture yourself kneeling before Jesus. Imagine him feeling the pain in your heart. What do you think he would say to you? What would you like for him to say?

THE FACE OF LONGING

ART CONTEMPLATION

Turn to illustration 3 and take several minutes to contemplate Jesus' face of longing.

Describe your reactions to the interaction between Jesus and this man.

Where are your eyes drawn?

In what way do you identify with the connection between Jesus and this individual?

As you study the face of Jesus, how would you describe his expression? How does his face make you feel?

CHAPTER THREE

THE FACE OF LONGING

The LORD longs to be gracious to you;
he rises to show you compassion.
—Isaiah 30:18 NIV

When I was in first grade, one of our neighbors, who was in college studying education, did a report about me for one of her classes. I remember Sherry coming over, playing games, and giving me simple tests to perform. I thought it was great fun, and I felt special that she chose me for such an important assignment. I suspected that there must be something unique, even remarkable, about me for Sherry to have chosen me as her subject. At least, until my mom read me the report.

I saw it in a folder on our coffee table and asked her to read what it said. My main recollection was the stinging comment by Sherry that, "I would describe Beth as a very average child." For some reason those words stuck with me. From that point on, I felt labeled as dull, lacking any distinguishing features. In my mind, I was the poster child for common—just plain vanilla. That is, until I discovered a special aptitude.

The summer after fourth grade, I began to play the French horn. I chose this instrument after a brass quintet had come to our school and performed. The sound of the French horn enthralled me. (My parents weren't overly thrilled: "Couldn't you play the flute or something!?")

To my surprise, and to my family's, I began to demonstrate a natural ability for music and for this instrument. In turn, that caught the eye of my most-beloved teacher, Mrs. Carson. She was my elementary school music teacher, a woman with an uncanny ability to inspire students to love music.

One day, I took a music test for which I hadn't studied. As a result, I did poorly—I got a C-, as I recall. Mrs. Carson called me back to her desk and asked what I thought of my grade. I felt embarrassed, and so I answered her dishonestly and said that I thought it was fine.

Mrs. Carson looked at me with sincerity tinged with disappointment and said, "I think you are capable of better." I will never forget that moment. Her words both stung and complimented me; she was longing for more from me and calling it out.

THE MESSAGE ON A FACE OF LONGING

Can you picture what it looks like to see longing on another person's face? It's a complex expression. It can be a mixture of tenderness and sadness, belief and disappointment, desire and pensiveness.

Longing is a powerful emotion. John Eldredge, in his book *The Journey of Desire*, describes it this way: desire is "the essence of the human soul, the secret of our existence. Absolutely nothing of human greatness is ever accomplished without it."

To understand the power of longings, consider what the world would be without them:

- There would be no more longing to create: no new movies made, pictures painted, books written, or songs composed.
- There would be no more longing for human connection: no new friendships cultivated, hospitality extended, couples married, or families started.

- There would be no more longing for God: no one seeking after God or engaging with Christ's purposes in the world.

To live is to long, and when we stop longing, we stop living. We experience a failure to thrive.

The Bible tells us that God longs. His yearnings reveal his deepest desires for us and prompt his movement toward us. Isaiah 30:18 says that "the LORD *longs* to be gracious to you; / he rises to show you compassion" (NIV, emphasis added). In the Gospels, Jesus looked out over a forlorn crowd of people and said that he longed to gather them under his wings as a hen would gather her chicks. Paul said that we often don't know how to pray for ourselves, but the Holy Spirit intercedes for us with longings too deep for words (Romans 8:26, paraphrased).

JESUS' FACE OF LONGING

Can you envision Jesus' face with an expression of longing—a look that sees right into your heart, wanting to call out from you your very best? When we experience Jesus' yearning, we witness his earnest resolve for us. Sometimes that's uncomfortable, especially if what he wants for us isn't what we want for ourselves.

In the Gospel stories, Jesus looked into the eyes of a Samaritan woman who had been married five times, and who was living with a sixth man who was not her husband; and Jesus wanted more for her. He looked at the crowds who gathered to have their bellies filled, and he ached to feed them more than a simple meal. He looked into the eyes of a nighttime visitor, Nicodemus, and craved to give him more than answers to his questions.

Jesus longs for us to embrace the life he knows we are capable of and to live by values that matter to his kingdom. If we could see his face, it would be full of passion, just as it was the day a certain young man came to see him with something important on his mind (see Mark 10:17-22).

LONGING FOR WHAT WE MOST NEED

While spending time in a Judean region east of the Jordan River, a number of parents brought their little children to Jesus for his blessing. The disciples, irritated by these parents' request, chided them for interrupting Jesus' itinerary. When Jesus found out, he was indignant! He scolded the disciples for missing the whole point: "Let the children come to me. Don't stop them! For the Kingdom of God belongs to those who are like these children" (Mark 10:14).

Jesus blessed the children profusely and then went on his way. As he started toward Jerusalem, suddenly a man came running toward him: a young, regally dressed, distinguished man, a ruler of some sort (Mark 10:17-22).

He surprised Jesus and the disciples by immediately sinking to his knees before Jesus—an unexpected posture for a man of his social rank. And then he spoke: "Good teacher," he asked, "what must I do to inherit eternal life?"

Jesus, intrigued with his address, returned a question. "Why do you call me good? Only God is truly good." Then he studied the young man and responded the way this youth likely expected. Jesus listed a number of the Ten Commandments and suggested that he obey them. Then, Jesus watched to see his reaction.

The young man looked with disappointment into Jesus' face. He protested, "I've obeyed all these commandments since I was young."

Then Jesus penetrated his gaze and looked straight into his heart. "Looking at the man, Jesus felt genuine love for him" (Mark 10:21). Jesus was overcome with a profound longing to relieve this young man's frustration. He responded with tenderness to the intensity on his face and the confusion in his eyes.

"There is still one more thing you haven't done. . . . Go and sell all your possessions and give the money to the poor, and you will have treasure in heaven. Then come, follow me" (Mark 10:21).

The young man looked back at Jesus with shock and defeat. He felt pricked and exposed. Jesus had put his finger on "it"—the very thing that covertly occupied the affections of his heart. Yet, the cost of giving up his wealth was overwhelming. He walked away, downcast, pained to have Jesus name his obsession and to realize that he didn't have it in him to give up his wealth.

EXPOSING FALSE SYSTEMS

This man was working his plan, yet his plan didn't seem to be working. The "rich, young ruler," as he is called in many translations of this Gospel story, had it all; yet he knew that something was missing. He came to Jesus, as many of us do, because of an inner emptiness and unrest, a spiritual void.

This young leader was doing everything he knew to do to gain favor with God and satisfy his spiritual hunger, yet the sensation persisted. Something was missing. So, he decided to come to Jesus, thrust himself at Jesus' feet, and ask for advice.

Jesus wisely responded to his question, "What must I do to inherit eternal life?" by proposing the very rules the young man had been following to try to inherit eternal life. He had been doing everything he knew to do. So Jesus said, "*Do* some more."

Jesus wanted him to feel frustrated. He yearned for this young man to see that his way of trying to achieve acceptance with God wasn't offering him what he truly needed. Jesus pressed him to consider that maybe his system was broken.

Jesus desires to expose the false systems we trust in to make life work. He dreams of the day when we become more childlike and experience life as a gift, gladly and innocently receiving his generous acceptance. He prefers the words *enter* and *receive*, rather than *do* and *inherit* when referring to life in the Kingdom.

AFFIRMING THE GOOD, SEEING POTENTIAL

Mark's account of this story notes that Jesus took a long, steady gaze at this young man and felt genuine love well up. Even in the midst of this man's troubled soul and misguided thinking, Jesus saw something beautiful and good. He saw earnestness; the presence of true desire, so genuine and clean that it made Jesus smile. Certainly, this young man was a performer, impressed with himself, and a tad self-righteous. But deep inside, Jesus saw his honest quest for love and his true need for God.

When Jesus looks into a heart with a wistful gaze, he is able to sort through the hodgepodge of mixed desires to affirm what is good and pure. He wants more, yet accepts what is. He sees potential, though embedded in problems. He doesn't negate the good simply because we aren't *all* good.

Understand—holy longings are not impatient or irritable. They don't shame a person into changing. They accept people where they are while still wanting more for them. As in the story of my music teacher, desires like this sting and inspire.

INVITATION FOR RELATIONSHIP

Jesus' advice to the young nobleman ended with the invitation to come and follow him. This invitation might have gotten lost, overridden by the titanic advice to lose all his wealth and give it to the poor. But it really was the point and climax of Jesus' recommendations!

This young man believed that the best he could hope for was to enjoy the wealth he had and to work really hard to be a good person by following the laws of Moses. Then he would make it to heaven, where he hoped life would have more meaning.

Sound like anybody you know?

Jesus was overwhelmed with love and yearned to walk alongside this youth as he found his way into the kingdom of God. Jesus wanted this man to know him as his teacher and friend. His invitation to "Come, follow me" wasn't a nice afterthought. It was the most profound desire Jesus had for this earnest seeker.

True, life-giving, holy longings drip with desire for relationship.

THE HEART BEHIND A FACE OF LONGING

If the expression of longing is a mirror of Jesus' heart, what does it say about him? It says that he has the markings of a true friend. Only people who care deeply for us have dreams for our lives. Only people who are real confidants want us to experience all that is our potential.

There is no one who believes in you more than Jesus. He created you; he knows you completely; he is your biggest fan. And he brims with imagination for your life—a life that fits your most authentic way of being.

THE TRANSFORMATION FROM A LONGING FACE

The story of the rich, young ruler is peculiar to the Gospels because it is one of the few stories where the main character leaves Jesus' company sad. Truthfully, we don't know how things end. All we know is that this man left Jesus dampened in spirit. But maybe that wasn't such a bad thing.

When we experience another's longing, we sometimes confront stubborn places in our heart, where we lack desire for our ultimate good. When I told Mrs. Carson that I thought a C- was just fine, she expressed her wish for me, the belief that I could do better. I had to wrestle for a time with whether I believed I could do better *and* whether I wanted to do better.

The transformation from experiencing another's longing may be the impetus we need to realize our potential and make positive changes. Feeling sad is an okay step in that direction.

REFLECTING JESUS' FACE OF LONGING

When we experience the vision Jesus has for us, we are built up. Though his longings may address gaps in our lives between where we are and where we could be, his desires assure us that, with his help, we will get there. He believes in us.

Mirroring Jesus' face of longing to others can have the same effect. It is one way that we encourage others to realize their possibilities. In this story, we learn from Jesus how to ask questions and reflect back to someone the prospect we see in them. We don't tell them just what they want to hear, but what they need to hear. We affirm the goodness and integrity we see, and we call it out.

Think of your family, friends, and coworkers: who comes to your mind as someone with whom you have insight to impart? What is it you envision for him or her? How can you affirm him or her?

EXPRESSING LONGING THROUGH AFFIRMATION

Michael grew up in a tumultuous home, enduring the chaos of having five difficult stepfathers over the course of his life. It wasn't until his early twenties that he learned the father he was named after wasn't even his biological father. His mother worked hard but made a meager living—barely above the poverty level.

Mike grew up with little encouragement to make something of his life, until one day, his best friend in eighth grade invited him to church. It was a small, storefront Pentecostal church—quite a contrast to his nominal experience as a Roman Catholic.

This church was different, though. Mike felt nurtured here in a way that was foreign to him and for the first time experienced the love of Christ. Before long, this church became his surrogate family, a place where he belonged and felt supported.

Then everything began to change. Michael started caring about the dreams and desires he had for his own life. And he even discovered something he never knew about himself; he found out that he was smart.

At the beginning of eighth grade, Mike had been placed in a remedial English class. But by ninth grade, he was in honors English. And when he graduated, he was the valedictorian of his class!

During his high school years, one of the people who influenced Michael most was his English teacher. Mike's junior year, this teacher took initiative toward him and affirmed the potential she saw in him. He remembers her saying, "Mike, you have great ability, and it will take commitment and discipline to develop it."

During Mike's senior year, this teacher brought him home with her and helped him study for his college entrance exams. Because Michael had terrible acne, she even took him to a dermatologist, paying the bill herself. Together with her husband, a pastor, they took Mike to visit a college and arranged for an interview and a financial aid package that made it possible for him to go to college.

But when Michael went home and told his mother that he had been accepted into college and that his tuition would be paid, his mother refused to let him go. Brokenhearted, Michael went back to school and told his teacher. Together, the teacher and a school counselor took Mike to his house and helped him pack his bags (he was eighteen years old by then), so that he could live with his teacher and her husband for the summer.

That was a turning point. Michael began to see himself through God's eyes. He took authority for his own life. Mike went on to graduate from college, received his Master of Divinity degree from an Ivy League school, and has served as a pastor for more than thirty years.

Michael's life took a dramatically different trajectory because of the affirmations of his English teacher, someone in whose face he saw longing—longing for him to achieve his potential and to become the man she saw he could be.

IMAGINING PRAYER: BLESSING THE CHILDREN

As you think of Jesus' face, can you imagine what it would be like to see longing? Can you feel him look straight through you, into your heart, and name the good desires he has for you?

Let's return to the story of this rich, young ruler. Begin by spending a few moments in quiet, centering prayer.

- Then turn to Mark 10:13-22 and read it thoughtfully several times.
- Begin by imagining Jesus from afar as he scoops up these little children, holds them on his lap, kisses them on the tops of their heads, places his hands on them and blesses them. What is it like for you to watch him enjoy these children?
- Now picture Jesus getting up and moving on down the road. Imagine running to him, falling to your knees, and addressing him. What do you want to call him? What feels most natural to you?
- As you look at him, let him look deep into you. Feel his longing for you.
- Let him peer into your heart and name the good that gives him delight. Ask him what it is that he enjoys about you.

- Now, ask Jesus to tell you what he longs for you right now. What might he tell you is getting in the way?
- Pray for the strength to do whatever it takes to follow him.

QUESTIONS FOR PERSONAL REFLECTION OR SMALL GROUP INTERACTION

1. Take a moment, and in quiet prayer and reflection, ask God to bring to your conscious mind a time when, as a child, you felt the presence of God. Write about that experience.

2. When you think of someone who has a face of longing for you, who comes to mind? Describe that person.

3. Why do you think it was so important for this rich, young ruler to see Jesus?

4. How would you describe what the young man must have felt when he saw Jesus' face?

5. In the past, when have you experienced Jesus' longings for you, his gentle nudge or urging to grow into the person he created you to be? Explain.

6. Picture yourself coming up to Jesus on the road and kneeling at his feet. Imagine Jesus looking down at you. What do you think he would say? What would you like for him to say?

THE FACE OF HUMILITY

ART CONTEMPLATION

Turn to illustration 4 and spend several minutes contemplating Jesus' face of humility.

Describe your reactions to this scene of Jesus washing his disciples' feet.

Where are your eyes drawn?

How would you describe the mood of this scene?

As you study the face of Jesus, how would you describe his expression? How does his face make you feel?

1. THE FACE OF WELCOME

Let the Children Come
© 2006 Liz Lemon Swindle
Used with permission from Foundation Arts
www.foundationarts.com

2. THE FACE OF COMPASSION

3. THE FACE OF LONGING

Solomon, Simeon (1840-1905)
Christ and Youth, 1892 (w/c on paper)
©Private Collection. © The Maas Gallery, London, UK
The Bridgeman Art Library

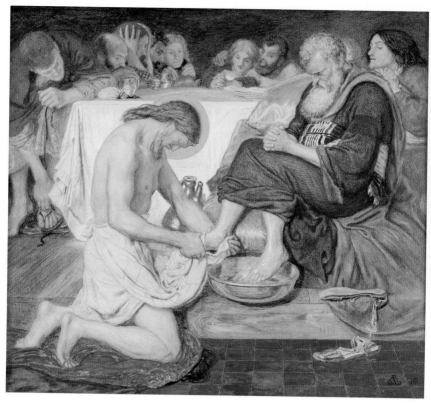

4. THE FACE OF HUMILITY

Ford Madox Brown (1821-93). Jesus Washing Peter's Feet.
1876 (oil on canvas)
© Manchester Art Gallery, UK
The Bridgeman Art Library

5. THE FACE OF SORROW

Carracci, Annibale (1560-1609). The Mocked Christ.
Photo: George Tatge, 1999.
Photo Credit: Alinari / Art Resource, NY
Pinacoteca Nazionale, Bologna, Italy

6. THE FACE OF INDIGNATION

Rembrandt Harmensz van Rijn (1606-1669).
Christ Driving the Moneychangers out of the Temple. 1634.
Photo Credit: Scala / Art Resource, NY
Pushkin Museum of Fine Arts, Moscow, Russia

7. COVER IMAGE

Rembrandt Harmensz van Rijn (1606-1669) (attributed to).
Head of Christ, 17th Century. Oil on panel, enlarged on all sides
9 3/4 x 7 7/8 inches (24.8 x 20 cm). John G. Johnson Collection, 1917.
Photo Credit: The Philadelphia Museum of Art / Art Resource, NY
Philadelphia Museum of Art, Philadelphia, Pennsylvania, U.S.A.

8. A FINAL ART CONTEMPLATION

Tissot, James Jacques Joseph (1836-1902).
Our Lord Jesus Christ, illustration for 'The Life of Christ,' c.1886-94
(w/c & gouache on paperboard)
Brooklyn Museum of Art, New York, USA
The Bridgeman Art Library

CHAPTER FOUR
THE FACE OF HUMILITY

Then Jesus said, "Come to me, all of you who are weary
and carry heavy burdens, and I will give you rest. Take
my yoke upon you. Let me teach you, because I am
humble and gentle at heart, and you will find rest for
your souls."
—*Matthew 11:28-29*

Pam walked through the doors of the women's prison, cradled within the pack of volunteers participating in a weekend ministry to inmates. She had never been inside a prison before. Her stomach knotted inconspicuously, a combination of curiosity and nerves.

The team received instructions on how to relate to the female prisoners. Pam listened attentively, not wanting inadvertently to cross a line. Pam's greatest concern was to listen to and value any woman she had the chance to meet—something my friend does with deep conviction and natural grace.

As she scanned the room, there were more than forty inmates in orange jumpsuits—sitting, standing, leaning— some in clusters and some alone. Pam noticed the talkative, outgoing ones as well as those who were more withdrawn. In the mix, one woman stood out to her among the collective orange assembly.

This woman was notably attractive, with the kind of beauty that would draw attention anywhere. She looked to be about Pam's age, in her late forties. What initially caught Pam's notice was the turned-up collar on her orange jump-suit—an ironic fashion statement.

It also struck Pam how typical she looked, as if she could be the neighbor next door or the shop owner down the street. Her demeanor reminded Pam of herself or one of Pam's friends. For a moment, Pam imagined herself in this woman's shoes and became curious to find out her story.

Pam learned that this inmate had been a prominent, well-respected businessperson in the community. What people didn't know was that she lived each day in a per-sonal hell, married to a degrading, abusive husband. Finally, after years of being humiliated and beaten down, the woman snapped. In a fit of despair and rage, she shot and killed him. Now she will spend the rest of her life incar-cerated in an oppressive prison of another kind.

This experience unsettled Pam. She felt deeply for all the women who lived in lockdown, stripped of virtually all their personal freedom. The thought of having that as one's destiny was overwhelming to her. Finally, she formed the thought that had been taking shape inside her: Pam real-ized that no matter who we are, we are all one poor choice away from prison.

Pam was articulating the core attitude that forms humil-ity within a person's being. It takes shape through two per-spectives: how you view yourself and how you view yourself in relation to others. A humble person recognizes the potential in all of us for horrific evil, as well as uncom-mon good. He or she would readily admit, "I am just as sus-ceptible as anyone to making poor judgments and committing rash acts that could send me to jail."

THE MESSAGE ON A HUMBLE FACE

Pam is one of the most accepting individuals I know. I never feel judged by her, nor do I observe her being unduly critical of others. Instead, she always sees the potential for goodness in people. Even when someone blows it, she isn't demeaning, but instead she extends grace and acceptance.

You might think that I'm describing Pam's personality—I'm not. Humility is often confused with traits like being mild-mannered, timid, or shy. Those are features describing someone's temperament. However, you can be a bold, vivacious individual who is also truly humble.

Humility isn't the same as poor self-esteem, either. It has nothing to do with frailness of personhood. Humble people have deep inner strength, resistant to the seduction of pride and self-inflation. They possess a healthy self-love without lifting themselves above others.

The word *humility* literally means "to be brought low," as illustrated by this verse: "Prepare a pathway for the Lord's coming! . . . Fill in the valleys and level [or humble] the mountains and hills!" (Luke 3:4-5, adapted).

Applying this concept, humble people never elevate themselves above others, but level themselves to an equal stature. That's what Pam did when she related to the female inmate. Pam identified with this woman and recognized her own potential to be in this woman's place.

The message humble people convey toward others is an attitude of mutual respect and acceptance. When you are in their company, you never sense a stance of superiority or aloofness. You don't feel concerned with whether you measure up to their standards. Instead, you enjoy being their equal.

Who comes to your mind when you think of a humble person? How would you describe that person?

JESUS' FACE OF HUMILITY

One of Jesus' most natural expressions is an attitude of mutual respect and acceptance. Stories in the Gospels certainly portray him that way. Jesus fascinated people who were typically on the margins of society, those most often devalued and disrespected within first-century Jewish culture. The list included Gentiles and Samaritans; women and children; tax collectors and sinners; the sick and demonized.

Rather than avoid Jesus, a group of motley characters gathered around Jesus, finding him attractive and enjoyable. This observation tells us a great deal about what it was like to experience Christ personally. His emotional effect was magnetic and disarming. Jesus put people at ease.

Women are a good example. Jesus rattled the cage of his culture in the way that he related to women. In Luke 8, the Gospel author names a band of female followers who traveled with Jesus and his twelve male disciples as he ministered around Galilee. Some of these women were married, and all of them had experienced healing through their encounter with Christ. They participated in ministry with Jesus, and he taught them. They were his bona fide disciples—a designation uncommon to women in his day!

To appreciate fully the modest demeanor of Jesus, we have to consider his relationship with the twelve followers who were his closest friends and disciples. These individuals were working-class, uneducated, common men. Several fished for a living, one was a tax collector, and the others we know little about. This sundry group of men became the little band of followers in which Jesus invested himself.

One particular scene portrays the down-to-earth nature of Christ poignantly: the time when Jesus disrobed, leveled himself, and washed his twelve disciples' dirty feet (John 13:1-38).

SEATED AT THE PLACE OF HONOR

As Jesus and his disciples gathered in the upper room, the Passover celebration at hand, his mood was heavy, his thoughts preoccupied. Knowing that the time had come for him to live out his most climactic act of love, he meditated on this moment with great thoughtfulness.

The table, laden with food, was low to the ground with

thin cushions surrounding it. Each of the twelve took his spot, Jesus in the place of honor at the head. John, a tender comfort to Jesus during this time, sat close, sensing his teacher's sadness.

The men carried on conversations with one another, subconsciously aware of the heaviness of this unnamed grief, the premonition that they were attending a farewell party and that something was about to happen over which they had no control.

Their upper bodies leaned forward toward the table, their left hands supporting their weight. They ate with their clean hands as they engaged in banter, their legs and sandaled feet extending behind them. Quietly, Jesus slipped back from the table. The eyes of his disciples glanced toward him, observing his quiet movement.

Jesus began to disrobe, taking off his outer garments and setting them aside. A large towel lay by the table, one that a servant had left behind. Jesus picked it up and wrapped it around his stripped body, mimicking the look of a lowly servant.

Jesus found a large bowl and poured water into it from a jug. Then he carried the bowl over to the table, stooping low to the ground behind each disciple. Taking on the job of a menial houseboy, one by one, he began to wash each of his disciples' feet.

The men felt awkward and uncomfortable. It occurred to some that they had failed to think about this simple act of hospitality—washing feet. Whose responsibility should it have been? Certainly none of theirs. Where was that servant who had prepared the food and thoughtlessly overlooked this courtesy? Their faces undoubtedly reddened with embarrassment, as they submitted to Jesus' act of cleansing.

They were silent, all except Peter. He never could use self-restraint when it came to questioning what Jesus was doing. With indignation, Peter protested, saying to him, "Are you really going to wash my feet?" Jesus insisted, responding to Peter, "Unless I wash your feet, you won't be able to share with me in this fellowship of servanthood" (John 13:6, 8, author's paraphrase).

Stunned and humbled, Peter consented, begging to be washed from head to toe.

CLOTHED IN HUMILITY

When Jesus shared in this meal with his disciples, he wanted it to be memorable—a teachable moment. His act of washing their feet was a foreshadowing of what was to come. Jesus, knowing that his earthly ministry was almost over, faced his final act of humility. He would submit himself to death on a Roman cross.

He chose to teach his disciples through this pericope—a smaller story germinating in the larger story of God's redemption—an unforgettable lesson about servant leadership.

The first thing Jesus did was take off his priestly robes, lay them aside, and put on the stole of a servant. Imagine being at a private dinner party and the guest of honor taking off his dress clothes and putting on an apron in order to bus the tables. Something about that act would seem inappropriate, out of place, and objectionable. That's how it must have felt to the disciples, as they watched their Lord put on the garments of a slave and perform an unbecoming task.

Humble people are like that. They don't mind taking on a lower standing than what life could afford them. Unpretentious people don't mind doing the chores that nobody wants to do. Their joy isn't in being lifted up, but in lowering themselves in order to serve others.

THE POSTURE OF THE HUMBLE

Jesus knelt as he made his way around the table behind each of his disciples, washing and wiping their feet. His posture reflected the essence of humility, the idea of leveling oneself to the stature of those with whom you are relating.

In this society, only the lowliest of servants would engage in such an undignified job. Even peers would not offer that act of service to one another. The disciples could hardly imagine washing one another's feet, let alone allowing Jesus, their teacher, to wash theirs.

After Jesus was finished, he asked the disciples if they understood why he did what he did. He brought up the fact that they referred to him as "Teacher and Lord," and, he affirmed, rightfully so. Jesus explained that his act of washing their feet took nothing away from his authority and personhood as their Teacher and Lord. Instead, he served them out of the fullness of his personhood, and he now admonished them to do the same.

Humble people don't cling to their titles as proof of their value or worth. They don't have to include their credentials with their signature, or mention them in order to remind others of their importance. People who possess true meekness throw off those designations while freely and willingly stooping to love, serve, and honor others. They are secure, knowing that to do so, they lose nothing of their own self-worth.

HUMBLE TO THE NTH DEGREE

It was a common courtesy in Middle Eastern culture for servants to provide jugs of water and basins for foot washing. The roads in Palestine were dusty and coated their sandaled feet. Though people would bathe their bodies early in the day, their feet became dirty from walking wherever they needed to go.

However, not all servants would have actually done the washing of feet, but simply provided the resources for individuals to do their own cleaning. Only the lowliest class of servants would have performed the act of foot washing.

Jesus astounded his disciples when he modeled humility to the *n*th degree by performing this debasing act. He drew no line in terms of how far he would go to serve. No job was too humiliating or beneath him.

In our day, only the truly self-effacing volunteer to clean toilets, pick up garbage, change dirty diapers, and care for the sick and dying—all those jobs that involve sights and smells that are repulsive. Humble people's senses are assaulted, just the same, but they don't let that override their impulse to act out of the meekness in their heart.

HUMILITY IS NO CHOOSER OF PERSONS

Gathered around the table were Jesus' closest male companions. He had other disciples, women and men, who traveled with him and participated in his ministry. But these twelve were the men whom Jesus had specifically chosen to lead the revolution after he was gone.

John was seated on one side of Jesus, Peter close by. And somewhere in the mix was Judas. John, who told this narrative in his Gospel, mentioned that Judas had already made plans in his heart to betray Jesus.

As Jesus made his way around the table, he was cognizant of what was in Judas's heart. In fact, after he had finished washing all their feet, including Judas's, Jesus became deeply troubled and emotional, asserting, "I tell you the truth, one of you will betray me!" (John 13:21).

Can you imagine washing the feet of someone whom you knew was about to betray you and have you killed? The truly humble don't sift through the crowd, choosing the ones they will serve and the ones they won't. Humble people serve their enemies. Harder yet, humble people serve those who pretend to be their friends.

THE HEART BEHIND HUMILITY

The heart behind Jesus' humility was love, without agenda. Because he was genuinely meek, his acts of servanthood were not manipulations offered for the express purpose of changing someone. They were sincere acts of regard, expressing Jesus' deep respect and affection for humankind.

Jesus honored his friends as he poured cool water over their feet, cradled their feet in his lap, and dried them off. You can imagine Jesus cherishing each man as he silently, graciously served him. This foot washing was an act of beauty rooted in a heart full of esteem and appreciation for his friends.

THE TRANSFORMATION FROM A HUMBLE FACE

The point of Jesus' act of lowly service wasn't lost on the disciples. There was nothing subtle about it. They got the message, especially John. Every Gospel writer included an account of the Last Supper, but John was the only Gospel writer to include this story of Jesus washing his disciples' feet. For such a singular and paramount event, it's curious that only John mentioned it. It obviously left a big impression. Perhaps it was because he found Jesus' actions excruciatingly poignant.

Just weeks before, John, along with his brother James, had cornered Jesus with a special request. They asked for a particular privilege in Jesus' kingdom: "When you sit on your glorious throne, we want to sit in places of honor next to you, one on your right and the other on your left" (Mark 10:37). John must have blushed, thinking back to that earlier conversation in light of this moment, his feet a damp reminder.

John and James received from Jesus the nickname "Sons of Thunder" (see Mark 3:17). It was a term of endearment, shedding light into the impetuous, competitive, bullish nature of these two brothers. Coupled with their brazen jockeying for position in Jesus' kingdom, this nickname showed that John had the makings of an arrogant, brash, upwardly mobile disciple.

Or at least you'd think so, until you read John's three short epistles to the church at Ephesus, written toward the end of his life. These letters reveal the tender, seasoned character of an old man, humbled by the love of Jesus. The servant heart of Christ thoroughly converted John.

A story from the end of John's life serves as a good illustration. According to tradition, John lived to be a very old man; and at the end of his life, when his disciples had to carry him in their arms to church, he would utter very few words except these: "Little children, love one another."

Jesus' servant leadership snuffed out John's ambition for greatness and his competitive drive. There was no need to prove himself, to raise himself above the other disciples or anyone else. Healed of striving, John was content to be "the disciple Jesus loved" (John 13:23).

REFLECTING HIS FACE OF HUMILITY

Humility is a by-product of seeing yourself realistically as someone possessing innate goodness while being a culpable, predisposed sinner. That foundational perspective informs the way you see yourself in relation to others—as equals, no higher and no lower.

As you meditate on the humility of Christ and experience his respect and regard for you, you will develop the attitudes that foster humility toward yourself and others. Jesus' value of you will help you have the courage to accept yourself and the grace to accept others.

Who in your life do you struggle to respect? Is there anyone who makes you feel disrespected? Imagine that person (or those persons) standing in front of you. If humility means "to be brought low or level," picture yourself at the same level, able to look him or her in the eye. Ask Jesus to heal your heart and empower you so that you neither elevate yourself above nor lower yourself beneath this person. Pray for and imagine mutuality between you.

EXPRESSING HUMILITY THROUGH SERVING THE LEAST OF THESE

My mother spent the last weeks of her life on a medical floor within a nursing home. Because of her declining health, Mom could no longer live alone and required constant medical attention.

One evening, while I was visiting with Mom and her roommate, Betty, another resident wheeled herself into the room. Betty was an amputee, and this woman was a recent amputee, as well. She had come to ask Betty to help her put on her prosthetic leg.

I watched from my side of the room as this woman winced, laboring with Betty to pull the thick rubber end over her stump. After several minutes of struggle, she looked up at me and asked if I would come and help.

My insides flinched, as I gulped down apprehension and went over to help her pull the band over her little, bald nub. I thought to myself, *I've never done this before. Oh, God, I need your help.*

I felt my "humility deficit," as I swallowed hard and did what she asked me to do. At the same time, I was also very aware of the goodness of serving her. I knew I was caring for her as Jesus would.

It takes practice to begin relating from a place of deference toward others—to express love that is without an agenda. One of the best ways we learn meekness is through serving someone Jesus called "the least of these"—people on the fringes, the invisible and voiceless.

The elderly and the dying certainly fall into this category. It isn't merely doing something kind or helpful for them. It is seeing them differently, as people with dignity and value.

You grow from treating them with respect and receiving the gifts they have to offer you.

IMAGINING PRAYER: LETTING JESUS WASH YOUR FEET

When you imagine Jesus, do you picture him having a humble countenance? Do you envision feeling comfortable with him, completely known and respected by him?

- Return to the story of Jesus washing the disciples' feet. Take time to read John 13:1-38, thoughtfully and slowly.
- In your imagination, envision yourself seated at the low table, on a cushion, with your feet behind you. (You may even want to take this position physically.)
- Feel Jesus approach you from behind and begin to bathe your feet with cool water. Imagine his hands tenderly touching your feet, rinsing them, and gently patting them dry. Soak in the sensation of Jesus serving you through this affectionate act.
- Turn to him, look into his face, and experience his demeanor. Feel his humble countenance as he serves you. Ask him to wash your heart and mind as well.
- Listen to him and see what he has to say. Let his humble face heal you of your own striving.
- Rest, contented by Jesus' love for you.

QUESTIONS FOR PERSONAL REFLECTION OR SMALL GROUP INTERACTION

1. Take a moment, and in quiet prayer and reflection, ask God to bring to your conscious mind a favorite dinner you have shared with people important to you. Describe that experience.

2. When you think of someone who has a humble countenance, what person comes to mind? Describe that person.

3. Why do you think Jesus washed his disciples' feet? Why was this important for him to do?

4. How would you describe what the disciples felt when they experienced Jesus washing their feet?

5. In the past, have you envisioned Jesus with a humble face? Explain.

6. Picture yourself at the table you envisioned earlier. Imagine Jesus walking up behind you and stooping to wash your feet. What do you think he would say? What would you like for him to say?

THE FACE OF SORROW

ART CONTEMPLATION

Turn to illustration 5 and take several minutes to contemplate Jesus' face of sorrow.

Describe your reactions to this image of Jesus.

Where are your eyes drawn?

How would you describe this interaction between Jesus and the man?

As you study the face of Jesus, how would you describe his expression? How does his face make you feel?

CHAPTER FIVE
THE FACE OF SORROW

Sorrow is better than laughter,
because a sad face is good for the heart.
—Ecclesiastes 7:3 NIV

MIXED MESSAGES

I was visiting a church a few years ago, when the worship leader stepped forward to begin the service. In his opening comments he mentioned how hard it was to watch the news, referring to a recent bombing in London's subway system. His honesty and realness arrested my attention.

Then unexpectedly, he made an abrupt turn. He continued his commentary on the sorrows beleaguering our world with this perplexing statement: "But just remember: we don't need to be sad because we have Jesus!"

When did having Jesus become equated with not needing to be sad?

Why do we think it more spiritual to be a happy Christian than a sad one? After all, prophecy described Jesus as "a man of sorrows, who is well-acquainted with suffering."

We have an aversion to feeling sad, and so it follows that we may dislike picturing Jesus sad. Nevertheless, ponder for a moment what Jesus' experience of suffering worked into his life. Through his profound sorrow and encounter with pain and loss, his eyes have deepened with tenderness and understanding toward us and the nature of our human drama. Shouldn't that attract us to Jesus?

THE MESSAGE FROM A FACE OF SORROW

Adversity can actually soften a person's face. Have you ever known someone who had hardship in his life and you could see it in his eyes? Something was there that hadn't been before: a sweet, tender sadness.

When I think of a face transformed through suffering, I think of my dad's. He was the oldest of three sons and had all the first-born personality traits. He was a high achiever in school, a type-A personality; and at the age of thirteen he began to bench press the weight of the world. His father died tragically, leaving him in charge of his two younger brothers and mother.

During World War II, he became a pilot and flew a B-24 bomber on several missions over Italy. When the war was over, he went to college and earned a degree in pharmacy. His later careers were in sales. No matter what Dad did, he was successful and accomplished.

My dad had a robust personality that kept his vulnerabilities tucked deeply inside. He was extroverted, yet not necessarily relational. At times he could be aggressive and bullish, hard to work with, and tough on weakness when he saw it in others.

Don't get me wrong: I loved my dad and I knew he loved me. Yet, I often didn't feel safe with him; I wasn't able to be myself or let down my guard. That all changed, however, when he was diagnosed with terminal cancer.

We found out that Dad had only twelve to eighteen months to live. I couldn't imagine how he would handle becoming weak and frail. He had always been a self-made man—competent, capable, on top of his game.

However, to my surprise, he handled it very nobly. Over

the months, as he became increasingly frail, I saw him accept the disease and its ultimate outcome. Through his letting go, all his tough, outer, hard case was sloughed off, and his gentle heart was exposed.

During Dad's last couple of weeks, when he was bedridden and a sack of bones, I would come to him, lean over, and softly say, "Hi, Dad." His eyes would open, dipped in a soft, grey-green sweetness, and he would say, "Hi, Sissy."

A new depth and tenderness filled his eyes, residue from his firsthand experience with profound grief and pain. Suffering changed him and our relationship as well. Through his painful journey, Dad's heart became accessible.

Ecclesiastes 7:3 makes a peculiar claim that, "Sorrow is better than laughter, / because a sad face is good for the heart" (NIV). How can that be? In my experience, pain is a specialized tool that can pulverize the hard, outer shell that we construct to protect our hearts from becoming vulnerable and experiencing hurt. Once that casing is gone, recovery of our true, genuine hearts begins.

Obviously, not all who suffer undergo positive transformation. Some who grieve internalize a bitterness that you can read in their eyes. You sense hardness of heart and livid anger just beneath the surface. They refuse to accept and surrender to the pain life has brought along, and it shows on their faces. The impact of adversity can go either way.

But when anguish has softened a person's face, he or she becomes more trustworthy. Stripped of ego and arrogance, people who suffer may become more human and real. You look into their war-torn eyes and know that you can trust them because of their humble, available heart. They join the "fraternity"—a band of souls who have accepted the transforming grace of becoming broken.

SORROW ON THE FACE OF JESUS

For those who met Jesus, there must have been an unmistakable mark of sadness in his eyes. Perhaps not all the time. Looking deeply, I imagine a deep-set melancholy, which spoke of his lonesome vigil as the Suffering Savior of the world.

Jesus had numerous life experiences that acquainted him with the emotion of sorrow. Although there were several, anguish indelibly marked the period between his betrayal and crucifixion. During this interval, Jesus experienced intense distress as he surrendered to one painful loss after another, each one bringing him a step closer to death (see Matthew 26:17-46).

THE END OF A GOOD THING

As Passover approached, Jesus and the disciples prepared to share this anticipated meal together. Peter and John had gone into Jerusalem and met a servant with a water jug (just as Jesus told them they would), who led them to a home. When the two disciples arrived at the home, they asked the owner where they might share the Passover meal with Jesus; and he took them to a large, upstairs guest room, where everything was set up. It was in this room that they arranged for Passover.

Soon, the others joined them, including Jesus. He looked tired, with dark circles under his eyes that alluded to long days and short nights of sleep. Something else was apparent, as well. He seemed preoccupied—a bit far away.

Once they sat down around the table, Jesus' face brightened as he told them how much he had been looking forward to being with them, sharing in this meal together. He said it would be his last meal with them until the fulfillment of its meaning in the kingdom of God (see Luke 22:16). The disciples weren't certain of all that Jesus meant, but they could tell that his words were measured. Quickly, the tone of the supper turned from a celebration to a farewell party.

Then, Jesus took some of the bread on the table and thanked his Father for it. He tore it into pieces and passed it around for the disciples to share. As they each tasted a pleasant morsel, Jesus explained that the bread was a symbol of his body that would be broken for them.

Then Jesus took the cup, thanked his Father for the goodness of its contents, and passed it around, encouraging each to drink from the common cup. He savored the pungent aroma, explaining that this would be the last time he would taste the fruit of the vine until the Kingdom of God had come.

After supper, Jesus took another cup, cradling it in his palms and pondering it. He slowly studied his friends' faces. "This cup," Jesus said, speaks of "the new covenant between God and his people—an agreement confirmed with my blood, which is poured out as a sacrifice for you" (Luke 22:20). The men were silent and thoughtful. Together, they lingered, drinking in the intimacy of this sacred moment.

SAYING HIS GOOD-BYES

One can only imagine the agony Jesus felt as he looked at each of the men whom he had poured himself into for three years and knew that he was leaving. Jesus understood that from that point on, nothing would be the same. He was saying good-bye to these dear friends and returning to his Father. As much as he longed for reunion with his Father, he felt a sting in his heart as he sat with his disciples for their last meal together.

One of the common ways we suffer in this life is through having to accept the ending of something good—when we have to say good-bye or see a pleasurable chapter of life come to a close. If we're in the midst of a dreadful time, we're happy to see it end. However, when relationships are sweet and life is good, it is depressing to know that this period of life will soon be over.

Jesus' time with these men had been good. They had laughed and played together, had adventures and worked hard together, and talked deeply. A true bond of friendship had formed. This was his first drink of sorrow from the cup of suffering.

SUFFERING FROM THE WOUND OF A FRIEND

His eyes milky, his tone a gentle somberness, Jesus proceeded: "But here at this table, sitting among us as a friend, is the man who will betray me" (Luke 22:21). An incredulous silence ensued.

How could this be? These were his closest, most intimate companions. To imagine one of them selling out Jesus was inconceivable. Each privately wondered of the others, *Is it him?*

They sang a hymn together and left for the Mount of Olives, a familiar place where Jesus would pray. On their way, Jesus, aware of their heightened suspicion of one another, confided that this very night, all of them would desert him. This admission destabilized not only each man's trust of the others but also his trust of himself.

In particular, this assertion got under Peter's skin. He quickly defended himself and said that even if everyone deserted Jesus, he wouldn't. Jesus responded with a gentle correction. He told Peter that even before the morning rooster had a chance to crow, Peter would deny three times that he even knew Jesus.

Betrayed by Judas, deserted by his closest friends, and denied by Peter, Jesus' heart was breaking. Abandoned by the ones he had loved so much and so well, he felt overwhelmed by all the hurt.

Those who suffer this kind of injury attest that the wound of betrayal feels like a dagger run straight through the heart. It is one thing when an enemy does harm to you. But to suffer the betrayal of friends is an awful and excruciating blow. There are no words to express the pain, and there is no place to contain it.

I will never forget the time a friend betrayed me. When I

saw him, right after he turned his back on me, I could see betrayal in his eyes. I intuitively knew what he had done. Frankly, the look I saw was so cold and sinister that even as I recall the memory today, it sends a chill down my spine and pains my heart.

Betrayal is a ruthless act. Desertion is cowardly. Denial is devastating. Jesus took a hit from each of these arrows— directly to the heart, another drink of sorrow from the cup of suffering.

THE ANGUISH OF SURRENDER

Jesus and the disciples arrived at the olive grove, also called Gethsemane, around 10:00 or 11:00 p.m. On the night of Passover, it was a common custom for Jews to stay up late, reminiscing over former days in Egypt when the angel of death had "passed over" the Israelite homes while taking the life of every first-born Egyptian son (see Exodus 11).

Once they arrived, Jesus asked Peter, James, and John to come pray with him in a secluded spot in the garden. He told them, "My soul is crushed with grief to the point of death. Stay here and keep watch with me" (Mark 14:34).The Gospel writer Luke tells us that Jesus was in such extreme agony, that his sweat fell to the ground like great drops of blood (see Luke 22:44).

The three watched, sleepily, as Jesus went on a little further, dropped to his knees, and poured out his anguish and turmoil in prayer. James and John heard him ask, "Abba, Father, . . . everything is possible for you. Please take this cup of suffering away from me. Yet, I want your will to be done, not mine" (Mark 14:36).

There it was again: the cup of the new covenant, the cup of suffering.

They watched Jesus collapse under the turmoil of surrendering his will. He felt the agony in his body and soul—he hated to feel pain. Yet, Jesus adored his father and wanted desperately to do his will. He quaked with ambivalence, wanting and not wanting, yielding and despising the awful-ness of death.

Jesus didn't feign being a stoic. Instead, he fully embraced the anguish of drinking the cup.

THE HEART BEHIND A FACE OF SORROW

If the sorrow on Jesus' face mirrors his heart, what does it tell us about him? It clearly projects his long-suffering love for us, a devoted affection so patient and determined that he willingly subjected himself to pain and loss for our sake. He surrendered to death in order to forgive us. He accepted becoming human in order to accompany us through our own human experience.

The unnamed author of Hebrews has amazing insight into the purpose of Jesus' suffering. He or she wrote that Jesus wanted so much to identify fully with our creaturely condition that he was willing to experience all the strains and stresses of that state. As a result, "Since he himself has gone through suffering and testing, he is able to help us when we are being tested" (Hebrews 2:18). Consequently, Jesus doesn't offer us theoretical advice when we face our own adversity; he joins us in it as a compassionate and understanding friend.

To whom do you go when you are in trouble, or when tragedy or trials come your way? Don't you turn to people you know can relate to what you're going through? It's peo-ple who can draw empathy from the well of their own tra-vail and heartache who become safe companions along the pathway of suffering.

THE TRANSFORMATION FROM A FACE OF SORROW

That evening, when the disciples saw the depth of sor-row in Jesus' eyes and read the lines of torment on his face, they knew he had the capacity to feel every pain that had ever pierced their own hearts. When they looked at him and saw overwhelming sadness, they understood what it required of him to yield to death for their sake.

Their Last Supper together, the bread and cup, and the time in the garden were unforgettable experiences. Afterwards, the disciples could instantly recall the expressions on Jesus' face, his grief over leaving them, and his terrible agony in Gethsemane. Every time they remembered these events, they comprehended more fully the depth of his love for them and his capacity to accompany them when they entered their own Gethsemanes.

And they did—eventually. Tradition tells us that ten disciples were martyred on Christ's behalf—all except Judas, who hung himself after he betrayed Jesus (see Matthew 27:3-5) and John, whom some believe died as an old man while exiled on a remote island. What transformed the disciples from deserters and deniers to loyal-unto-death disciples?

Jesus' courage and willingness to suffer for their sake transformed them. His sacrificial life inculcated bravery to face their own deaths. Overwhelmed by Jesus' love, they comprehended that following Jesus meant laying down one's life. They understood that discipleship involved a price tag. Consequently, they willingly surrendered themselves to the ultimate sacrifice.

Often we are shocked and dismayed to discover that following Christ requires deprivation. We fall prey to the notion that knowing Jesus should guarantee a blessed life protected from pain and loss. However, for our Suffering Savior to transform us, our paradigm of discipleship must change: we must accept the reality that following Jesus will often lead us *toward* sacrifice.

REFLECTING HIS FACE OF SORROW

When Jesus experienced and expressed sorrow, he simultaneously legitimized the emotion. He said it was okay to be sad—counter to the worship leader's opinion. We do others and ourselves a great disservice when we reject heartache and unhappiness as valid sentiments. These feelings are gifts from God, given to help us process life.

Until we expand our hearts to feel the pain of life, we reinforce the disconnect between real life and our acknowledged experience of life. In other words, we pretend. We pretend that we're not hurt, that we're okay, that we have moved on from trying times.

Our world is in dire need of real people who model a genuine way of grieving the losses of life. You will become an agent of healing when you learn to live authentically with your own sadness and express it in valid, honest ways to others.

Who do you know who is distressed right now? What life experiences have equipped you to understand his or her pain? As you open yourself to Jesus, your Suffering Savior, and experience his empathic presence, you will be better equipped to bear the sorrows of others.

EXPRESSING SORROW THROUGH LAMENT

A few years ago, during a seminar that I attended on inner healing prayer (see end of section), I was asked to be involved in a live demonstration of an exercise called a "lament." The presenter asked me to write about a painful memory, using raw, emotional language to help me feel the hurt of this ungrieved loss. I did so, recalling a situation when I was bullied and disparaged by some people.

That evening I wrote the description, and the next morning I read it to the presenter and the fellow seminar participants. It was an emotional and unnerving experience to read such deeply personal reflections. However, as I have learned from the past, it often takes risk for God to access a wound and bring healing to the heart.

As I began the process of sharing this lament, not surprisingly, the Spirit of God began to minister to me in the place of hurt that remained. Through tears, I read the story of what it was like for me, describing the injury, anger, betrayal, and helplessness I felt. After I finished reading, but still in a mode of prayer, the leader suggested that I ask Jesus where he was when all of this happened.

So, I asked Jesus—and instantly, a thought entered my conscious mind: *I was there with you all along; and every arrow you took, I took with you.* I didn't contrive the thought; I simply, instantly knew it. And I knew what Jesus meant.

He didn't mean that he vicariously felt my pain or merely empathized with me. Jesus meant that he took every arrow as if it entered him! He helped me understand that whenever we attack another human being, created in the image of God, we are attacking him.

Then the caregiver encouraged me to ask Jesus what else he wanted to say. As I posed the question, again a thought immediately came clearly to mind: *What they were attacking in you—was me.*

I wept, streams of tears running down my cheeks.

Again, I understood what Jesus was saying. He wasn't telling me that I was right and they were wrong, that he was on my side and not on theirs. Jesus was telling me that because he lives in me, when they attacked me, they were attacking him in me.

Through this beautiful exercise of writing a lament, my Savior, who suffered with me through one of the darkest times in my life, met me in my grief. I am convinced that I wouldn't be where I am today in my healing if he had not done his work in my heart.

Would you be willing to ask God to show you if you have buried any ungrieved losses in your life? When you do, if a memory comes to mind, I recommend that you ask a caregiver, counselor, spiritual leader, or mature friend to accompany you in your lament.

Begin by writing down the memory in as much detail as you can. It is important to have the time and space to re-enter the wound and feel the pain of it. Capture that sensation with "level one" language: use raw, guttural, "deep-within" words. You may find yourself using words you don't often use to let out the anguish. Don't worry. Jesus can handle it.

Once you have written your lament, meet with your friend or caregiver right away and, in prayer, share it with him or her and Jesus. Ask this person to pray with you and for you, as you embrace and release the hidden sorrows in your heart. Ask Jesus where he was when this happened. Ask him if there is anything he wants to say.

As you learn to grieve effectively, you will reap a deepening of intimacy and freedom with Christ, and you will be better prepared to accompany others along their own healing journey. (I attended the healing prayer seminar at Ashland Theological Seminary. Dr. Terry Wardle was the presenter and created the exercise of lament. For more information, contact Ashland Theological Seminary, Formational Counseling Institute.)

IMAGINING PRAYER: THE LAST SUPPER

Envisioning Jesus as a man of sorrows will help you to embrace your own pain. In prayer, return to the story of the Last Supper. Read Matthew 26:17-46 thoughtfully and slowly.

- This time, enter the story, becoming one of the disciples seated at the table with Jesus. (You may even want to use real bread and wine or juice as you practice this imagining prayer exercise.)
- Picture yourself seated at a low table close to Jesus. Where are you in relationship to him? Are you across from or next to him?
- Now, imagine Jesus looking at you with sweet sadness in his eyes, as he breaks a piece of bread off and gives it to you. Take the bread and taste it; savor it in your mouth. Hear him say, "This is my body, broken for you."

- Then Jesus picks up the cup and extends it to you. Take it from him and sip. Let the pungent taste fill your mouth, awakening your taste buds, the fragrance wafting over you. Swallow the liquid slowly as you hear him say, "This is my blood, shed for you, for the forgiveness of your sins." Receive his body and blood into you. Let it cleanse and purify you completely and thoroughly.
- Look into his eyes, deep pools of kindness and love, softened by his own suffering. Experience the fellowship of him suffering with you and for you. Stay there with Jesus for as long as you like. Rest. Heal. Be loved.

QUESTIONS FOR PERSONAL REFLECTION OR SMALL GROUP INTERACTION

1. Take a moment, and in quiet prayer and reflection, ask God to bring to your conscious mind a time when you experienced profound sorrow. Describe that experience.

2. When you think of someone's face that has been softened because of sorrow, who comes to mind? Describe that person.

3. What do you think it was like for Judas to eat the Passover meal with Jesus? What was it like for Jesus to eat the Passover meal with Judas?

4. How would you describe what Peter, John, and James must have felt when they saw Jesus' face in the garden of Gethsemane?

5. In the past, have you envisioned Jesus with a face of sorrow? Explain.

6. Picture yourself in the garden with Jesus. What would that have been like for you? What would you have said or done?

THE FACE OF INDIGNATION

ART CONTEMPLATION

Turn to illustration 6 and take several minutes to contemplate Jesus' face of indignation.

Describe your reactions to this scene of Jesus driving out the money changers from the temple.

Where are your eyes drawn?

In what way do you identify with this expression on Jesus' face?

As you study the face of Jesus, how would you describe his expression? How does his face make you feel?

CHAPTER SIX
THE FACE OF INDIGNATION

He looked around at them angrily and was deeply sad-
dened by their hard hearts. Then he said to the man,
"Hold out your hand." So the man held out his hand,
and it was restored!
—Mark 3:5

IRON JAWED INDIGNATION

The Nineteenth Amendment to the United States Constitution provides that neither any individual state nor the federal government may deny citizens the right to vote on the basis of their gender. Today, the fact that an amendment was necessary to secure this right seems unequivocally absurd. Yet, history reveals that countless women endured intolerable suffering to win this basic human right.

The 2004 film *Iron Jawed Angels* tells the extraordinary story of a group of determined and courageous individuals who put their lives on the line to fight for American women's right to vote. Led by Alice Paul (played by Hilary Swank) and her friend Lucy Burns (played by Frances O'Connor), the film captures the formidable force of resistance the group faced.

In one scene, police arrest an assembly of women picketing outside the White House on the premise that they are obstructing traffic. Refusing to pay a fine for a crime they didn't commit, the members of the group are sent to a women's prison for sixty days. Conditions are so deplorable that in protest, Alice Paul begins a hunger strike.

The warden of the prison, through a torturous method, attempts to force-feed Paul and others who join the hunger strike—thus winning the women the nickname "iron jawed angels." Finally, after secretly releasing a written description of the appalling conditions of the prison and the inmates' treatment, they generate enough attention to force these activists' release and their eventual pardon.

Because of the tenacity of Alice Paul and several other valiant comrades, on August 26, 1920, the Nineteenth Amendment to the U.S. Constitution—also known as "the Susan B. Anthony Amendment"—became law, and 20 million American women won the right to vote. People who were vexed by inequitable laws against women instigated this dramatic historical shift. Indignation fueled their protest—an outcry that finally arrested the attention of our nation and overturned history.

The emotion of indignation is somewhat difficult to describe. It is a complex brew—mixing anger, sadness, and outrage—most often directed at something believed to be unfair, unreasonable, or just plain wrong!

Provoked, an indignant person will often do the unthinkable: cross the picket line, place himself or herself in the line of fire, sit down on the bus, or refuse to eat. This individual's stubborn resolve simply put says: "I've had enough!"

One can distinguish indignation from anger because of the tint of grief, sadness, or hurt. It is often not merely a "personal" affront but more far-reaching in scope, directed particularly at issues of cruelty or discrimination.

THE MESSAGE OF AN INDIGNANT FACE

When we feel indignant, we are protesting a violation of some sort. This emotion requires the ability to hang on to one's temper while feeling angry and perturbed. Offended, the indignant person doesn't lash out to avenge or harm another, but feels the insult of the dignity of life and expresses it in consternation.

Rosa Parks, as a black woman, was indignant that laws prohibited her from sitting down at the front of the bus after a long day. Finally, she had enough! In protest, she took a seat up front in an act of quiet defiance.

The message we read from this expression of indignation is convicting. It says, "I won't play by these rules any longer." Indignation reprimands injustice, confronts duplicity, and convicts heartlessness. When we experience another's righteous anger, though we might feel fearful, it isn't so much for our own physical well-being as it is for our exposure. His or her face pierces the self-serving, self-righteousness of our own heart.

JESUS' FACE OF INDIGNATION

As you study the expressive nature of Jesus, you will notice that he displayed a full range of human emotions, including anger and indignation. His colorful palette of responses reveals a fully alive inner life. He took in the world and allowed it to affect him.

The scenes that capture his indignation are numerous. Once, when parents brought their children to Jesus for his blessing, the disciples shooed them away. Jesus was indignant and scolded the disciples for their obtuse notion that children were of no consequence to him.

When entering the temple, accosted by the carnival atmosphere of merchants buying and selling religious goods and services, he was repulsed! Fashioning a whip, Jesus drove them out, knocking over tables and chairs, and creating a scene.

The people most often the object of his sorrow-filled anger were the hyper-religious in town. The Pharisees and scribes became the object of many of Jesus' tirades against duplicitous, sanctimonious religiosity. "You are so careful to clean the outside of the cup and the dish, but inside you are filthy—full of greed and self-indulgence!" (Matthew 23:25).

Jesus expressed indignation: he railed against the traditions of men that inhibited the protection of those who were young, old, poor, innocent, helpless, and oppressed. One such individual was a man with a mangled hand. During a Sabbath gathering in the synagogue, with the religious leaders present, Jesus saw this man and, moved with compassion, called him forward (see Mark 3:1-6).

CARING TO NOTICE

He was a regular at the synagogue, though typically he hung back in the crowd, the reproach of his deformity obvious to all. As the service began, Jesus, an itinerant rabbi, was introduced. Before Jesus said anything, the disabled man had a premonition that Jesus would call on him. It brought back memories of school, when the teacher's eyes bore a hole through him, exacting a response. His heart began to pound.

Jesus motioned for him—an informal gesture—to come forward. Everything in him protested. He hated to be the object of attention, let alone set before the entire worship assembly! He wanted to say no, but the awkwardness of the moment prevailed.

Moving to where Jesus stood, the man looked into Jesus' face, and found Jesus' determined tenderness looking back. Jesus had cared to notice him—not because he had done anything to draw attention to himself. He hadn't come to request anything special. He was there, as usual, and Jesus saw him.

Those who respond to injustice and unfairness in the world do so because they care enough to notice. They aren't recruited to become involved—they feel their way into the fray. Violations of human dignity rub their hearts the wrong way.

Not long ago, I had the privilege of hearing Parker Palmer speak. As an author and insightful thinker, Palmer has provoked the conscience of American educators for more than thirty years. He brings a vital message—the need to repair one's soul with one's role.

He posed the question, "What vexes you?" To be vexed is to experience an irritation over some issue before you. Palmer went on to explain the importance of noticing what "vexes" us because "that thing is where we must move in order to engage in our life work."

So, what vexes or irritates you? What issues loom big and unconscionable, evoking your own indignation?

CONFRONTING THE REAL ISSUE

Indignation has a way of cutting through the external paraphernalia to get to the real issue. Jesus, sensing his enemies' eyes watching his every move, brought the man before those assembled. The Pharisees sat with hands piously stroking their beards, feigning interest.

But Jesus knew their hearts. Cold and calculated, they waited for Jesus to break a law so they would have grounds to arrest him. He threatened them and threw off the equilibrium of their religious systems. He challenged their power. And so they sat, patiently waiting for the right time to accuse Jesus of some fabricated infraction.

Jesus didn't act coy but turned right to them—all eyes in their direction. Now they began to squirm, feeling the set-up of something over which they had no control. Jesus looked straight through into their hearts and asked, "Does the law permit good deeds on the Sabbath, or is it a day for doing evil? Is this a day to save life or to destroy it?" (Mark 3:4).

Frozen by his gaze, a flammable mixture of hot anger and cool indignation, they sat, unwilling to respond. However, the cat-got-their-tongue reaction didn't faze Jesus. He continued to stare—expressing righteous anger at their hardness of heart toward their fellow pilgrim. Indignation has a way of cutting through to the core and exposing attitudes that foster arrogance and apathy.

INDIFFERENT TO THE COST

Jesus "looked around at them angrily and was deeply saddened by their hard hearts" (Mark 3:5). Then he turned to the trembling man and beckoned him to hold out his hand. Instantly, Jesus restored it completely! The gathering gasped in awe; the Pharisees seethed with their own sordid indignation.

They were offended, angry that Jesus would toy with them and their religious legalism. How dare he stir up questions of Sabbath protocol? Their rage was a pathetic, egotistical defense mechanism. Jesus challenged their authority and their superior spiritual edge. And for that, he would pay. The Pharisees left the synagogue quickly, intent on one thing: forming a plot to end Jesus' life.

Jesus knew it was only a matter of time before he crossed the line of no return. Angst had been building. Fully aware of the Pharisees' growing resentment, this Physician proceeded to fulfill his purpose to heal the sick. He paid attention to what vexed him and acted defiantly in response to it.

Those who embrace their indignation learn quickly that it costs to speak up. They can't contain the ire in their hearts. A person who expresses this form of "righteous anger" puts himself or herself out, willing to risk for the sake of what is right.

Over my lifetime, the patronizing and demeaning of women has deeply vexed me, especially in the church. On numerous occasions, with eyes wide open, I have watched pastors and leaders promote a message that men and men alone possess unique spiritual authority. And, on numerous occasions, I have paid the price for speaking out.

THE HEART BEHIND INDIGNATION

As Jesus expressed indignation, what heart attitudes predisposed him to feel this fury? First, he experienced this emotion from his deep love for righteousness. Whatever polluted and marred goodness, or opposed and hindered the values of God's kingdom violated Jesus' heart.

Second, Jesus wanted to please his Father more than he wanted to please men. His loyalty to his Father superseded the natural, human instinct for self-protection. Jesus had such a deep, uncompromising love for God that he took on anything that offended his Father's heart, no matter what it cost.

TRANSFORMATION FROM AN INDIGNANT FACE

To be on either end of the stick of indignation isn't pleasant, whether experiencing it or receiving it. However, this expression has properties to transform us in very critical ways. It's the "whistleblower" emotion, awakening us to damaging conflicts of interest going unchecked in our world.

It took the fortitude of Sherron Watkins, former vice president with Enron Corporation, to blow the whistle on Enron's unscrupulous business practices. Others, of late, have followed in her steps, prompting the development of protective legislation for people who stick their necks out to expose fraud, corruption, waste, or environmental hazards.

In some ways, indignation describes the biblical term *conviction*—a pricking of conscience from the Holy Spirit, drawing attention to unresolved wrongdoing. When we experience a situation that provokes indignation, often God's Spirit within us is the culprit, blowing God's whistle on wrongs that need to be righted.

REFLECTING INDIGNATION

Something significant happens in us when we learn how to hang on to ourselves in anger. Our soul expands, and we release creative energy. We learn new discipline: the art of feeling the offense without attacking the offender. We develop greater honesty, acknowledging the fury and grief of our angst while reflecting it with frank and uncompromising dignity.

Paying attention to what perturbs you is formative to living with a conscience in our world. If you are willing to think critically, to feel negative energy, indignation will change you and may even change history! As you meditate on Jesus' angry response to issues that vexed him, his outrage will empower you to reflect the same righteous fury toward situations that call for change. In so doing, you may even discover an invitation to your life work!

A word of caution: indignation is not a license for self-righteous, arrogant judgment of others. We direct indignation toward the indefensible wrong of injustice, a transgression to God's heart. In so doing, that doesn't make us "superior."

EXPRESSING INDIGNATION THROUGH EXPOSING INJUSTICE

Most relate the provocation of the Civil War to the leadership of Abraham Lincoln over the issue of slavery. However, if you were to have asked Lincoln who incited the war, he might have given you the name of a woman: Harriet Beecher Stowe.

Stowe wrote the acclaimed novel *Uncle Tom's Cabin*, a poignant exposé about the lives of black slaves and the cruelty of their owners during the mid-1800s. She candidly described the slaves' life of bondage, disclosing their plight and exposing their story. Using colloquial dialect and vivid detail, Harriet Beecher Stowe led the reader to experience life as a slave. While the novel has been criticized in recent times for its depictions of the behavior and speech of its black characters, other contemporary scholars have focused on the impact of the novel at the time of its publication and acknowledged its historical importance in the area of race relations in the United States.

In its first year, *Uncle Tom's Cabin* sold more than 300,000 copies! Many historians, and some have said even Lincoln himself, credited this book as the match that lit the fire of indignation toward slavery in our country. By frankly describing the injustices done to slaves, Stowe pricked the conscience of many Americans, and after a bloody civil war, the United States abolished slavery.

It's obvious that Harriet Beecher Stowe never dreamed when she wrote *Uncle Tom's Cabin* that it would incite public outcry and lead the way toward the abolishment of slavery. More than likely, she simply wrote about what vexed her. When we pay attention to what disturbs us, we discover proactive ways to express indignation toward social injustices and bring about reform.

So, what angers and irks you? What righteous cause raises your ire? Have you ever thought that perhaps that fire within you is Christ's indignation, loving the world through you and longing for its restoration? What will you do about it?

IMAGINING PRAYER: LETTING JESUS AWAKEN YOUR INDIGNATION

What is it like for you to picture angry indignation on Jesus' face? Can you envision his consternation without feeling afraid or full of shame?

Let's reenter the story, trying to imagine the scene. Begin by reading Mark 3:1-6 slowly and thoughtfully. Imagine yourself as the person in the story who has been afflicted, the person to whom Jesus seeks to bring healing.

- Picture the synagogue, filled with people. On one side, the Pharisees huddle together. The common people gather around Jesus, and you are in their midst.

- Imagine that Jesus sees you and calls you forward. By his look, he knows what it is that you are feeling. How do you feel disabled? What do you feel like hiding?
- What people in your life are like the Pharisees? Who has been heartless and indifferent to your pain? Name them to Jesus.
- Look into Jesus' face. See his hurt for you. Imagine his indignation toward those who have oppressed you. How does it feel to have Jesus defend you?
- Show Jesus the part of you that needs healing. Let him touch you.
- Keep your eyes focused on his beautiful face—full of loyal, uncompromising love for you. Be strengthened by his love.

QUESTIONS FOR PERSONAL REFLECTION OR SMALL GROUP INTERACTION

1. Take a moment, and in quiet prayer and reflection, ask God to bring to your conscious mind a time when you felt indignant about something. Write about that experience.

2. When have you observed indignation on someone's face? Describe the circumstances.

3. How do you think Jesus' indignation affected the man whose hand Jesus healed?

4. How would you describe what the Pharisees must have felt when they saw Jesus' face of indignation?

5. In the past, have you envisioned Jesus expressing indignation? Explain.

6. Picture yourself observing this scene between Jesus, the Pharisees, and this man. How would this interaction have affected you? Explain.

EPILOGUE

Christianity cannot survive in this world, or in our
own lives, without its mystical roots. In this sense,
mysticism is not the reception of extraordinary, miracu-
lous experiences. Rather, the mystic is one who is fully
alive in a vibrant relationship with God. The mystic's
God is not a distant, foreboding power, but the Intimate
One who is here and now.
—Stephen J. Rosetti

From my beginnings as a Christ follower, I have desired, perhaps even insisted, on having an experiential relationship with Jesus. I've had an aversion to overly intellectualized faith or rigid, self-righteous piety. Instead, I've longed for a keen awareness of Jesus. I've wanted real, mystical encounters with him.

Now, for those who might be uneasy with the terms *mystical* or *mystic*, let me (hopefully) reassure you. I use these words as in the tradition of Christian mysticism, a stream of Christianity dating back to the church fathers. Individuals such as Saint John of the Cross, Meister Eckhart, Theresa of Ávila, Thomas à Kempis, and C. S. Lewis are among those referred to as Christian mystics—people possessed by an insatiable hunger for the nearness of God.

I admit the challenges of having this proclivity. Many days, I yearn for a deeper experience of Christ and, frankly, don't have one. There have been seasons of life where I have weathered dry and dusty spiritual deserts.

Of course, over the years I have also grown in my awareness of the need for thoughtful, biblical thinking and the
necessity of being led by faith, not by emotionalism. Yet, I
still yearn for real encounters with the Intimate One. Times
of sweet, soul-satisfying communion with Jesus have left
such a profound and enduring impact, that I keep vigil for
more.

Picturing the Face of Jesus is a book intended to help Christ
become more real to you. I write with the conviction that
until Jesus is real, your faith will sag: it will be weak and
dispassionate, and your life will not resemble what it
means to live in the way of Jesus. *Radical faith is born of real
encounter.*

Through using the mediums of art contemplation,
gospel storytelling, and imagining prayer, my hope is that
you have been primed to engage with the living and ever-
present Christ. If that happens, I am overjoyed! The intent
of this book has been fulfilled, and God's longing for you to
seek his face has been satisfied.

OUR LORD JESUS CHRIST BY JAMES TISSOT

As you come to the end of *Picturing the Face of Jesus,* consider contemplating on one final image, illustration 8. This painting by James Jacques Joseph Tissot captures a penetrating expression on the face of Christ. Imagine what it would be like to stand in front of Jesus and look directly into his eyes. Take several minutes to study his face and demeanor. Then respond to the following questions.

Where are your eyes drawn?

How would you describe the expression on Jesus' face? What is he feeling?

What do you think he has on his mind?

How do you feel as you look deeply into Jesus' eyes?

What does it mean to you that Jesus has his hands placed over his heart?

Of all the images in this book, which one has affected you the most, and why?